The Correct Interpretations and English Translations of Tang Poems and Song Lyrical Poems

Accompanied with Calligraphy and Vernacular Chinese

唐宋詩詞正解並英譯
附書法白話

KS Vincent POON（潘君尚）

Kwok Kin POON（潘國鍵）

The SenSeis

First Edition
April 2025

Published by
The SenSeis 尚尚齋
Toronto
Canada
www.thesenseis.com
publishing@thesenseis.com

ISBN 978-1-989485-39-2

Cover
Hiroshima Castle Museum
廣島城博物館
Hiroshima Japan
by KS Vincent Poon

In Loving Memory of
Pui Luen Nora TSANG（曾佩鑾）

Table of Contents

Preamble I

This book provides concise and correct translations of several popular Tang poems (唐詩) and Song lyrical poems (宋詞), including those by Li Bai (李白, 701-762 AD), Bai Juyi (白居易,772-846 AD), Xue Ying (薛瑩,?-? AD), Su Shi (蘇軾, 1037-1101 AD), Li Qingzhao (李清照, 1084 – 1151 AD), and Lu You (陸游, 1125-1210 AD). Annotated line-by-line translations are presented in neat and simple words that are easy to understand, with each line's true meaning revealed by extensive research. Vernacular Chinese translations are also given. In addition, every poem is accompanied by Chinese calligraphy to enhance readers' appreciation of traditional Chinese culture.

Tang poems and Song lyrical poems are known for their elegant and straightforward language. Yet, Chinese interpretations often contain critical mistakes. Most English translations additionally suffer from excessive fancy language that is hard to follow. This book aims to fix all these maladies of arbitrariness, which is relatively common in both Eastern and Western academia.

Here, I would like to wholeheartedly thank my father, coauthor Dr Kwok Kin POON (潘國鍵博士), for his unreserved teaching and valuable contribution.

KS Vincent POON
April 2025, Toronto

Preamble II

唐宋詩詞解讀匡謬

潘國鍵

(一)

　　唐詩宋詞，世之瑰寶。惜時人解讀，多但憑所學，未必深究。殊不知詩詞正解，須下功夫。且引本書所錄，略舉數例以言之。

(二)

李白《江上吟》

　　木蘭之枻沙棠舟，玉簫金管坐兩頭。美酒尊中置千斛，載妓隨波任去留。仙人有待乘黃鶴，海客無心隨白鷗。屈平辭賦懸日月，楚王台榭空山丘。興酣落筆搖五嶽，詩成笑傲凌滄洲。功名富貴若長在，漢水亦應西北流。

(I)

　　白話正解對譯：在木蘭舷的沙棠船上，船頭船尾擺放著華麗的管樂器。酒罈裏面，盛置了千斛的美酒。載同歌妓，隨著波浪，任由木船去或留。仙人尚要依靠騎黃鶴，浪跡四海的我呢，卻就江上的白鷗也無心去跟隨。屈原作的辭賦，仍屬懸掛空中的日月；楚王建的高臺華榭，早已空空不在山丘。興盡酒酣剛下筆，五嶽為之立震搖；詩成時那種玩笑輕慢、狂放不羈，遠遠凌越住在歸隱的地方。功名富貴若是長存在，那漢水亦應(逆向)朝西北奔流囉!

(II)

「詩成笑傲凌滄洲」一句，坊間多譯作「詩成之後，嘯傲之聲，直凌越滄海」。誤。

蓋「滄洲」一詞，唐宋詩詞常見，多喻指自己屬意的避世歸隱之地。唐詩杜甫《曲江對酒》「吏情更覺滄洲遠，老大悲傷未拂衣」是也。宋詞陸游《訴衷情•當年萬里覓封侯》那句「心在天山，身老滄洲」，更是膾炙人口了。

按「滄洲」亦作「滄州」。劉長卿《送鄭說之歙州謁薛侍郎》有「老得滄州趣」、方干《白艾原客》有「滄州幾年隱」，李白別有詩《贈盧徵君昆弟》謂「滄州即此地，觀化遊無窮」，皆可為證。

「滄洲」、「滄州」，俯拾即是。不但再非地名，更且各有所寄。此吳融《雨後聞思歸樂二首》所言「我家方旅食，故國(故鄉)在滄洲」也。它又怎會是「滄海」呢？

此句白話該作：「詩成時那種玩笑輕慢、狂放不羈，遠遠凌越住在歸隱的地方。」

(三)

白居易《題玉泉寺》

湛湛玉泉色，悠悠浮雲身。閒心對定水，清淨兩無塵。手把青筇杖，頭戴白綸巾。興盡下山去，知我是誰人。

(I)

白話正解對譯：濃濃景色的玉泉寺，悠悠浮雲的閒適身。安閒的心，應答澄靜的水。清清淨淨，兩不染俗塵。手執青筇手杖，頭戴白綸絲巾。盡興之後下山去，管得我是什麼人！

(II)

「知我是誰人」，「知」多解作「知道」。誤。末句若僅著意俗眼「知道我是什麼人」，未免庸鄙，亦不合全詩格調。蓋詩之「閒心」、「定水」、「清淨」、「無塵」，意皆擺脫凡俗。結語「知我是誰人」，該是避世明志，亦為全詩點睛，宜好好細讀。

按白氏於公元815年作詩(i)，時值官場鬥敗，被貶江州司馬(ii)。對名利鬥爭與俗世眼光，已開始厭倦。詩中流露的，正是這種避世心態。此其一。復讀杜甫《鸚鵡》「翠襟渾短盡，紅嘴漫多知」、王維《桃源行》「坐看紅樹不知遠，行盡青溪不見人」、吳潛《八聲甘州•和魏鶴山韻》「如何是，一尊相屬，萬事休知」等句，則「知」當解作「管」也。此其二。是知「知我是誰人」釋作「(你)管得我是什麼人」，始為合適。

名利斷，六根淨。好? 壞? 哈哈，理得我!

(四)

蘇軾《念奴嬌•赤壁懷古》

大江東去，浪淘盡、千古風流人物。故壘西邊，人道是、三國周郎赤壁。亂石穿空，驚濤拍岸，捲起千堆雪。江山如畫，一時多少豪傑。　遙想公瑾當年，小喬初嫁了，雄姿英發。羽扇綸巾，談笑間、強虜灰飛煙滅。故國神遊，多情應笑我、早生華髮。人間如夢，一尊還酹江月。

(I)

白話正解對譯: 大江流水東奔去，浪水沖刷殆盡的、是久遠前一眾傑出人物。舊堡壘的西邊，有人說這就是、三國時周瑜(和曹操開戰) 的赤壁。江邊雜亂的石塊堆得聳若入空，震懾人心的波濤拍擊著岸邊，捲起了千堆雪般的浪花。江山美麗如畫，這時期確有很多豪傑。　遠想公瑾(周瑜)壯年，小喬剛嫁了給他，雄武才溢，神采煥發。從容自若、氣定神閒，談談笑笑之間、強暴的敵人(曹操)

就給他殲個灰飛煙滅。家國神遊，對它還如此癡情的該是、這已生白髮的可笑的我。 塵世如夢，倒不如帶酒一罐，敬向江上明月奠酒相對飲!

(II)

此詞「羽扇綸巾」，一般解作諸葛亮。誤。蓋前文既謂「周郎赤壁」、「遙想公瑾」，則「雄姿英發」句後之「羽扇綸巾」，在思路上沒理由突然來個諸葛亮。

檢南宋孝宗《賜虞允文辭免顯謨閣學士知平江府不允詔》謂虞允文:「羽扇綸巾，嘗掃舟中之敵; 輕裘緩帶，久宣塞上之勞。」(iii) 又謝逸《潛心堂》詩云:「羽扇綸巾延客晚, 蒲團禪板坐更深。」(iv) 是則「羽扇綸巾」用作「從容自若、氣定神閒」的替代語，宋代經已如此。兩宋以降亦然。例如元代周巽 《挽周宣慰方壺》詩有「羽扇綸巾雅量閒，梅嶺雲歸凱初奏」，邵亨貞《臨江仙•擬無住水檻過雨》詞有「羽扇綸巾閑到我，百年世事匆匆」之句; 明代沈采《千金記•登拜》戲曲亦有「得志也羽扇綸巾」之語。俱與諸葛亮本人一無關連也。

近讀南宋趙以夫 《漢宮春•次方時父元夕見寄》結語云:「應自笑，周郎少日，風流羽扇綸巾。」(v) 則蘇詞「羽扇綸巾」講的是周瑜，宋人已如是說。 大家還在嚕啥?!

(III)

蘇軾又曰「故國神遊，多情應笑我」。「故國」大多解作「三國時的赤壁戰場」，「多情」則為對此戰的「無限感慨」，俱未確當。蓋周瑜當日情場戰場兩得意，又怎生令人感慨? 若是傷己，那就太小家子氣了，不合蘇軾豪邁性格。

按「故國」一詞，唐宋文人慣語，多指故鄉。惟此處「故國」，除故鄉之外，猶帶「本國」之義。甚類丘遲《與陳伯之書》「見故國之旗鼓，感平生於疇昔」(vi)、周賀《出關後寄賈島》「故國知何處，西風已度關」所言之「故國」也。

考蘇軾謫居黃州，元豐五年(1082AD)七月中遊赤壁。九月宋軍於永樂城與西夏一戰慘敗，「喪士卒役夫二十餘萬」(vii)。神宗「涕泣」(viii)，朝野震動。此詞當事後蘇軾有感而作。所謂「懷古」，實則喻今。是以「故國」意指「本國」居多。而「多情」者，非深情故鄉又或赤壁，而實是情繫家國也。

蘇軾生活年代，江山雖依舊如畫，可悲者外患頻仍，屢屢敗績。國家既乏周瑜這等難得的將才豪傑，「強虜」(遼夏)也從來沒見「灰飛湮滅」。而朝廷則黨爭迭起，振興無望。對家國事務竟還如此癡情，實在可笑得很!

所以，若言全詞最精妙之處，當不在寫赤壁，也不在褒周瑜，更不在什麼得意失意，而在於一個「笑」字，─「我很可笑」。「多情應笑我」，亦應解作:「對它(家國)還如此癡情的該是這可笑的我!」

由於可笑，所以覺悟，悟了「人間如夢」。這正正道達了中國傳統有志文人對時局的那一種憂患卻又強烈的無力感，終難逃看破紅塵的宿命。不僅可笑，兼且可悲。

(IV)

至若「早生華髮」呢? 蘇氏寫的實是他當時發現自己生白髮了，開始老了，非謂早在年輕時便長白髮也。蓋「早」字可義為「已」，無關年齡。宋秦觀《阮郎歸‧退花新綠漸團枝》之「日長早被酒禁持」、元盧摯《沉醉東風‧閑居》之「早來到竹籬茅舍人家」，「早」不就是「已經」的意思了麼?

時人據此謂蘇軾笑自己早年生白髮，哎喲，算真如此，區區幾根白髮，蘇氏豁達，豈足興懷?!

(V)

又結語「還酹江月」，人多解作「把酒澆地以祭月」，亦未得其要。

「還」者，「還相 (輪流)」也，即《魏書‧楊津傳》記「洛周脫津衣服，...欲將烹之，諸賊還相諫止，遂得免害」(ix)之「還相」也。是以人與人相敬酒謂之「還酹」，宋人劉辰翁《須溪集》「有懷數友還酬一尊」(x)、明人吳寬《寄壽施煥伯七十》「少待登堂成一笑，手持春酒獻還酬」等句是也；人與物或亡靈相敬酒則謂之「還酢」，宋人何夢桂《赤壁夢鶴》「遼海千年約未寒，一樽還酢大江干(岸)」、元人耶律鑄《次韻閬州述事》「為誰携斗酒，還酢魯公祠」等句是也。俱有對飲之意。如是，「還酢江月」固非純屬向月奠酒，主要乃是與江月同飲。「一尊還酢江月」之句，當作「倒不如帶酒一罈，敬向江上明月奠酒相對飲」，方為正解。

唉，想蘇軾當時的心情會是: 笑我人間遲悟幻，放懷江月醉何難!

(五)

李清照 《一剪梅·紅藕香殘玉簟秋》

紅藕香殘玉簟秋，輕解羅裳，獨上蘭舟。雲中誰寄錦書來? 雁字回時，月滿西樓。　花自飄零水自流，一種相思，兩處閒愁。此情無計可消除，才下眉頭，卻上心頭。

(I)

白話正解對譯: 紅蓮花謝，竹席破舊，鬆開羅衣，獨自登上小舟。(夫君在)雲中(給金石迷住了，) 哪個會寄情書來? (他日)雁群飛回時，共賞月圓於西樓。　花自凋謝，水自流動，同樣相思，兩地分隔帶來無端的情愁。這相思愁情沒法可消除，—— 剛鬆下眉頭，卻立又湧上心頭!

(II)

「雲中誰寄錦書來」，「雲中」一般釋作「遠天白雲」之類，莫名其妙。

夫「雲中」者，實指雲崗石窟所在之石刻勝地宋「雲中府」(今山西大同)(xi) 也。考李清照夫君趙明誠情迷金石之學，著《金石錄》。李氏《後序》記其「窮遐方絕域，盡天下古文奇字之志」、「不能自已」(xii)。是知「雲中」當泛指趙氏往搜羅文物之外地，否則此句甚難通解。

在外地日夜搜羅，心無旁鶩。又怎會記得要寫情書給家中的妻子呢?!

(六)

李清照《臨江仙•庭院深深深幾許》

庭院深深深幾許，雲窗霧閣常扃。柳梢梅萼漸分明，春歸秣陵樹，人老建康城。　感月吟風多少事，如今老去無成。誰憐憔悴更凋零，試燈無意思，踏雪沒心情。

(I)

白話正解對譯: 庭院幽深多麼深，華窗高閣門常關。柳樹梢末、梅花蓓蕾漸都顯明，春天來臨，秣陵(建康)的樹活起來了，人(夫君)呢，卻已死在建康城。　受寒病重、吟讀古詩文，勾起很多(共研金石的)往事，(你)如今死去，事事無成。誰個可憐(我)容顏憔悴與衰頹? 預賞花燈無興趣，踏雪賞景沒心情。

(II)

此詞錯解最多。

把「人老建康城」解讀為李氏「看來要老死建康城」，「感月吟風多少事」解讀為李氏「憶往昔多少回吟賞風月，飲酒作詩，那是多麼幸福」，「如今老去無成」則解讀為李氏「如今卻人已老去，什麼事也做不成了」云云，逗人發笑。

所以犯錯，是因為沒讀懂「老」和「感月」之義。也忽略了李氏對古文金石也同樣癡狂。夫妻一起日夜醉心金石，是恩愛生活的主要部份，這是李清照在《金石錄•後序》自己說的。今天人們一讀見了「老」字，就判定必是李氏晚年之作，殊不知若讀《後序》所記，極大可能這是她葬夫後病重時寫的哀歌。

(III)

須知唐宋文人，頗把「老」字直作「死」字用。例如唐李賀

《牡丹種曲》「梁王(花)老去羅衣(葉)在，拂袖風吹蜀國弦」、子蘭《城上吟》「古塚密於草，新墳侵官道。城外無閒地，城中人又老」、譚用之《途中》「光陰老去無成事，富貴不來爭奈何」，又或上文所引陸游《訴衷情•當年萬里覓封侯》「身老滄洲」，「老」全是「死」、「逝」之意。

復據《後序》，夫婿趙明誠於建炎三年(1129 AD) 在建康(行在)病逝。所謂「人老建康城」，說的就是這回事，亦即「人死建康城」也。此詞大概作於趙氏死後翌年，即建炎四年(1130 AD) 的初春。字裡行間流露的，正是李氏「葬畢，余無所之」(xiii) 的孤悽心情。

由是，「人老建康城」、「如今老去無成」之「老」，皆非李清照將會「老死」，而是四十多歲年壯的趙明誠已經「病死」。

(IV)

至若更關鍵的「感月吟風多少事」一語，時人錯解「感月」為「弄月」，更覺離奇。是時李氏情緒極之低落，至於「試燈無意思，踏雪沒心情」，又何來心思去回味往日的「弄月」？

實則「感月」之「感」乃「感染」，「月」則代表「陰寒」。「感月」者，「感染寒涼而病倒」也。

考何休《春秋公羊傳注疏》載:

> 「言朝者，緣生以事死。親在，朝朝莫夕。已死，不敢褻鬼神，故事必於朔者。感月始生而朝。」(xiv)

勉強譯之白話:

> 「所謂『朝(問安)』呢，是緣照生前的禮法來事奉死後的父母。父母在時，每天朝早問安，傍晚拜見。死後，不敢褻瀆鬼神，故此事奉必在初一之日。若感染寒涼而病倒，始可依生前之禮去問安。」

復檢白居易《感月悲逝者》詩云:

「存亡感月一潸然，月色今宵似往年。」

又《皇明從信錄》載明武宗正德十六年(1521 AD)二月張岳上疏曰:

「近日聖躬偶感風疾，…偶爾感月，豈足過慮。」(xv)

皆明證也。

　　再據李清照《後序》所記，亡夫葬後，「余有大病，僅存喘息」(xvi)。是以「感月吟風多少事」，「感月」即「大病」無疑矣。喪夫兼大病，然後始有「誰憐憔悴更凋零」之句，寫的正是她當時的心境和病容。此詞作於建炎四年初春，即其夫歿後數月，不意又添一旁證焉。

　　又據《後序》，李氏夫婦藏有大量古籍與漢唐金石刻文，其中包括「寫本李、杜、韓、柳集」等等，少部份「搬在臥(室)內」，「偶病中把玩」。所謂「吟風」乃指此事，雖不中亦不遠。

　　此句解作「受寒病重、吟讀古詩文，勾起很多(共研金石的)往事」，方合。

(七)

李清照《武陵春•春晚》

　　風住塵香花已盡，日晚倦梳頭。物是人非事事休，欲語淚先流。聞說雙溪春尚好，也擬泛輕舟。只恐雙溪舴艋舟，載不動許多愁。

(I)

　　白話正解對譯:春風已息、微香殘留，花開已到了盡頭，日晝將盡，還是懶得去梳妝。景物依舊、人面全非，事事都罷休，正欲訴說，眼淚卻已先流。　聽說雙溪春色仍然好，也打算往那裡泛小舟。只恐怕雙溪舴艋細小舟，載的是它浮不動的許多(沈重的)哀愁。

(II)

「風住塵香花已盡」。「塵香」一詞，時人解作「塵土裡帶有花的香氣」。誤。

「塵」非「塵土」，應該是「塵輕」，亦即「輕微如塵」。唐聶夷中《古興》謂「片玉一<u>塵輕</u>，粒粟山丘重」是也。故「塵香」意即「微香」無疑，此亦宋明詩詞所常見。且舉四例：

(1) (宋)蘇軾 《元夕夜游絕句》：「午夜朧朧淡月黃，夢回猶有暗<u>塵香</u>。」
(2) (宋)吳文英《木蘭花慢•餞韓似齋赴江東漕幕》：「潤寒梅細雨，卷燈火、暗<u>塵香</u>。」
(3) (元)宋无《春愁》：「金雁(箏柱)<u>塵香</u>暗鳳絃,紅繩風緊閣秋千。」
(4) (明)楊慎《望西山》：「行行國艷皆桃李，處處<u>塵香</u>盡綺羅。」

上四「塵香」，全非「塵土」。是以此句該正解為：「春風已息、微香殘留，花開已到了盡頭。」

(八)

陸游《訴衷情•當年萬里覓封侯》

當年萬里覓封侯，匹馬戍梁州。關河夢斷何處？塵暗舊貂裘。胡未滅，鬢先秋，淚空流。此生誰料，心在天山，身老滄洲。

(I)

白話正解對譯：壯時志向萬里遠，覓取軍功獲封侯，(很想)單人匹馬前去戍守要地梁州。如今收復關中的夢醒了，此刻關中在哪？僅剩得一件滿佈塵埃、黯然無光的舊貂裘。 胡人還未消滅，顏鬢卻先衰老，淚是白流的了。怎料此生，心在抗胡的天山，身卻死在歸隱的地方！

(II)

「當年萬里覓封侯」。「當年」時人釋為「回憶當年」，誤。當為「壯年」。即《呂氏春秋•愛類》言「士有當年而不耕者，則天下或受其饑矣」(xvii) 之「當年」也。「萬里」時人釋作「奔赴萬里外的邊疆」，亦誤。「萬里」乃「志在萬里」，頗近「老驥伏櫪，志在千里」之「千里」，乃謂「志向遠大」也。

可歎陸游雖志向遠大，卻僅是一個「夢想」。下一句「匹馬戍梁州」，也只是他個人的「願望」。若讀《宋史•陸游傳》，什麼前赴梁州殺敵做大官，他從來就沒有實踐過。打後他寫的梁州詩句，例如《南定樓遇急雨》之「行遍梁州到益州」、《追感梁益舊游有作》之「梁州獵火滿秋山」，全是旅遊玩樂之作。時人竟把「戍梁州」作正史讀，也真奇怪!

由於這個錯誤，於是乎「關河夢斷何處」，就給解個一塌糊塗。甚麼「如今防守邊疆要塞的從軍生活只能在夢中出現，夢醒後不知身在何處」，讓讀者和陸游一起發夢去咧!

(III)

夫「關河」者，「關」是函谷關、潼關，「河」是黃河、渭水，俗謂「關中」，直《史記•蘇秦列傳》所記「秦四塞之國，被山帶渭，東有關河，西有漢中」之「關河」(xviii) 也。

陸游向來主張，要收復中原，須先取得關河(關中)。《宋史•陸游傳》載陸氏「以為經略中原必自長安始，取長安必自隴右始」(xix) 是也。他壯年夢想「戍梁州」，信亦因此。蓋梁州古漢中之地，宋興元府，治南鄭，今陝西南鄭縣治 (xx)。其地北制長安，南控漢水，歷來兵家必爭。陸游當然明白，無論攻復關河，抑或保衛江淮，都必先要守住梁州囉!

如是，「關河夢斷」意乃「收復關中的夢醒了」。「何處」意即「此刻關中在哪」。始確。

末句「老」、「滄洲」，上文 (六)(III)、(二)(II) 已各有析述，不囉唆了。

(九)

　　詩詞翻譯，原文務先解讀正確，否則譯來有何意義？本書英譯，皆吾兒君尚 (KS Vincent POON) 盡心之作，並附余之白話譯文。庶或略裨當世，啟迪來者。

二零二四年春七十五歲眇人潘國鍵撰於多倫多如心齋。由來同一夢，休笑古人癡。

<u>註釋</u>

(i) 朱金城，《白居易集箋校》。 上海: 上海古籍出版社，1988，
　　 p.355。

(ii) 劉昫，《舊唐書》卷166, 白居易傳。 臺灣: 臺灣中華書局，1971，
　　 pp.10-11。

(iii) 洪适 ，《盤洲文集》卷13 ，內制3。欽定四庫全書集部，乾隆
　　 四十六年版, p9b。

(iv) 謝逸 ，《溪堂集》卷4。欽定四庫全書集部，乾隆四十六年版，
　　 p4a。

(v) 唐圭璋 ，《全宋詞》冊4。北京: 中華書局 ，1999 ，
　　 p.3398。

(vi) 蕭統，《昭明文選》卷 43。崇文書局, 同治八年版, p19a。
　　 又姚思廉 ，《梁書》卷20 ，陳伯之傳。北京: 中華書局 ，1973
　　 ，p.315。

(vii) 陳邦瞻，《宋史紀事本末》卷9 ，「西夏用兵」。欽定四庫全書
　　 史部 ，乾隆四十九年版 ，pp.19-20。

(viii) 脫脫，《宋史》卷334 ，徐禧傳。臺北: 藝文印書館，乾隆武英
　　 殿版, p.4225。

(ix) 魏收,《魏書》卷58，楊津傳。北京:中華書局, 1974, p.1299。

(x) 劉辰翁 ，《須溪集》卷7。欽定四庫全書集部, 乾隆四十六版, p.48b。

(xi) 脫脫,《宋史》卷90，地理志 ，「雲中府」 ，見上, p. 1106。又臧勵龢,《中國古今地名大辭典》， 「雲中府」條。臺北: 臺灣商務印書館, 1966, p. 967。

(xii) 趙明誠,《金石錄》,書末李清照《金石錄後序》。欽定四庫全書史部, 乾隆四十一年版, p.1b。

(xiii) 仝上, p.4a。

(xiv) 何休,《春秋公羊傳注疏》卷13 。欽定四庫全書經部, 乾隆四十年版, p.20。

(xv) 陳建 ，《皇明從信錄》卷27，萬曆四十八年沈國元訂，冊9 , p.32。出版年地缺。

(xvi) 李清照 ，《金石錄後序》。見上, p.4b。

(xvii) 呂不韋 ，《呂氏春秋》卷21，「愛類」。浙江書局, 光緒元年版, p.9b。

(xviii) 司馬遷 ，《史記》卷69，蘇秦列傳。香港: 廣智書局, 出版年份缺 ，冊5，卷69，pp.1-2。

(xix) 脫脫,《宋史》卷395，陸游傳。見上, p.4873。

(xx) 《宋史》卷89，地理志，「興元府」。仝上 ， p.1093。又《中國古今地名大辭典》， 「梁州 」條。見上 ， p.814。又「興元府」條。全書, p.1234。

(完)

Li Bai
A Chanted Poem Upon a River

李白
《江上吟》

Calligraphy I

Calligrapher (書者): KS Vincent Poon (潘君尚)

Content (內容): *A Chanted Poem Upon a River,* a poem by Li Bai (李白《江上吟》)

Style (字體): Standard Script (楷書)

Caption (款識): 李白江上吟貳仟貳拾伍年潘君尚於多倫多尚尚齋 (Li Bai, *A Chanted Poem Upon a River*, the year of two-thousand and twenty-five, Kwan Sheung Vincent Poon scribed at Toronto's The Senseis)

Seal Inscription (鈐印): 君尚 (朱文) (Kwan Sheung Vincent, red characters), 潘氏 (白文) (The Surname of Poon, white characters)

Medium (材料): Ink on Xuan paper (紙墨水本)

Size (尺寸): 66 X 35cm

Year (年份): 2025

木蘭之枻沙棠舟玉簫金管坐兩頭

美酒尊中置千斛載妓隨波任去留

仙人有待乘黃鶴海客無心隨白鷗

屈平詞賦懸日月楚王臺榭空山丘

興酣落筆搖五嶽詩成笑傲凌滄洲

功名富貴若長在漢水亦應西北流

李白江上吟貳仟貳拾伍年潘君尚於多倫多尚尚齋

Calligraphy II

Calligrapher (書者): KS Vincent Poon (潘君尚)

Content (內容): A phrase from *A Chanted Poem Upon a River,* a poem by Li Bai (李白《江上吟》句)

Style (字體): Cursive Script (草書)

Caption (款識): 李白江上吟句潘君尚 (Li Bai, a phrase from *A Chanted Poem Upon a River*, Kwan Sheung Vincent Poon)

Seal Inscription (鈐印): 潘 (朱文) (Poon, red character), 君尚 (白文) (Kwan Sheung Vincent, white characters)

Medium (材料): Ink on Xuan paper (紙墨水本)

Size (尺寸): 67 X 44cm

Year (年份): 2023

仙人有待乘黄鹤，海客无心随白鸥。

李白江上吟句 癸卯 沈天昌

Translation

李白《江上吟》
Li Bai, *A Chanted Poem Upon a River*

木蘭之枻沙棠舟，玉簫金管坐兩頭。美酒尊中置千斛，載妓隨波任去留。仙人有待乘黃鶴，海客無心隨白鷗。屈平辭賦懸日月，楚王台榭空山丘。興酣落筆搖五嶽，詩成笑傲凌滄洲。功名富貴若長在，漢水亦應西北流。

白話對譯 Vernacular Chinese

在木蘭舷的沙棠船上，船頭船尾擺放著華麗的管樂器。酒罈裏面，盛置了千斛的美酒。載同歌妓，隨著波浪，任由木船去或留。仙人尚要依靠騎黃鶴，浪跡四海的我呢，卻就江上的白鷗也無心去跟隨。屈原作的辭賦，仍屬懸掛空中的日月; 楚王建的高臺華榭，早已空空不在山丘。興盡酒酣剛下筆，五嶽為之立震搖; 詩成時那種玩笑輕慢、狂放不羈，遠遠凌越住在歸隱的地方。功名富貴若是長存在，那漢水亦應(逆向)朝西北奔流囉!

English

1. 木蘭之枻沙棠舟，
The fragrant Mulan Magnolia (木蘭)[1] planks rest on two sides (枻)[2] of a Shatang wood (沙棠)[3] boat,

2. 玉簫金管坐兩頭。
All the luxurious wind instruments (玉簫金管)[4] lie on the two ends afloat.

3. 美酒尊中置千斛，
Jars hold thousands of cups (千斛)[5] of fantastic wines,

4. 載妓隨波任去留。
With the ladies of Song and Dance (妓)[6], I follow the waves to wherever the boat finds.

5. 仙人有待乘黃鶴，
While the Transcended (仙人)[7] still relies (待)[8] on riding a yellow crane (黃鶴)[9] to soar,

6. 海客無心隨白鷗。
I, wandering all over the world (海客)[10], have no intention of following the ivory gulls (白鷗) at all.

7. 屈平辭賦懸日月，
Qu Ping's (屈平)[11] Chu Verses (辭賦)[12] are still the brilliant suns and moons hanging high in the sky,

8. 楚王臺榭空山丘。
But the Head of Chu's (楚王) mighty terraces and pavilions (臺榭)[13] had long reduced to a void (空)[14] on the hillside.

9. 興酣落筆搖五嶽，
Overjoyed (興)[15] with drunkness (酣)[16], the Five Great Mountains (五嶽)[17] tremble as I begin to write,

10. 詩成笑傲凌滄洲。
With a poem composed, my contemptuous amusement (笑傲)[18] far exceeds reclusive delight (滄洲)[19].

11. 功名富貴若長在，
If fame and riches can stay forever set,

12. 漢水亦應西北流。
Then the Han River (漢水)[20] shall flow back to the Northwest.

(translated by KS Vincent Poon, November 2024)

Remarks

(I)

This poem was composed by Li Bai (李白, 701-762 AD), one of the most influential poets in Chinese history. According to some, it was composed around 759 AD[21], two years after his exile from the capital[22].

(II)

"滄洲" in the poem requires clarification. "滄洲" here is not a geographical location or "a great blue sea (滄海)"[23], as some suggested. Rather, it is a metaphor for "a place of reclusive delight (避世歸隱之地)".

A poet of Li Ba's era, Wu Rong (吳融, 850-903 AD), whose hometown was Yue Prefecture's Shanyi (越州山陰)[24], once wrote:

I. "本是<u>滄洲</u>把釣人, 無端三署接清塵."[25]
"I was originally a fisherman in <u>a place of reclusive delight</u>, so I have no intention of visiting the ministries to approach any dignitaries."
(translated by KS Vincent Poon)

II. "我家方旅食, 故國在<u>滄洲</u>."[26]
"My family indeed resides here as visitors now, but my hometown
resides at <u>a place of reclusive delight</u>."
(translated by KS Vincent Poon)

Similar usage can also be observed throughout prominent Tang
and Song literature, which include:

I. (唐) 杜甫《曲江對酒》: "吏情更覺<u>滄洲</u>遠, 老大悲傷未拂衣."[27]

II. (宋) 陸游《訴衷情•當年萬里覓封侯》: "心在天山, 身老<u>滄洲</u>."[28]

Thus, Li's "滄洲" is clearly a metaphor, not a specific fixed place
on Earth.

As an addendum, "滄洲" can also be written as "滄州", such as:

I. (唐) 劉長卿《送鄭說之歙州謁薛侍郎》: "老得<u>滄州</u>趣."[29]

II. (唐) 方干《白艾原客》: "<u>滄州</u>幾年隱."[30]

III. (唐) 李白《贈盧徵君昆弟》: "<u>滄州</u>即此地, 觀化遊無窮."[31]

Footnotes

(1) "木蘭" here refers to "a type of fragrant wood (香木名)". See
《漢語大詞典》. Shanghai: 上海辭書出版社, 2008, p.682.

(2) "枻" here refers to the "wooden planks on the two sides of a
boat (船舷)", as in《楚辭•九歌•湘君》: "桂櫂兮蘭枻, 斲冰兮積雪."
王逸注 : "枻, 船旁板也." Ibid., p.890.

(3) "沙棠" is "a type of tree whose wood can be used to build boats, and its fruit can be consumed (木名, 木材可造船, 果實可食)". Ibid., p.958.

(4) "玉簫金管" here serves as "a general term for luxurious wind instruments (泛指雕飾華美的管樂器)". Ibid., p.520.

(5) "斛" here is "a unit of volume measure (量詞)". Ibid., p.338.

(6) "妓" here refers to "the ladies of Song and Dance (歌舞女藝人)", as in 韓愈《順宗實錄二》: "癸酉, 出後宮幷教坊女妓六百人." Ibid., p.295.

(7) "仙人" is "a transcended person who has become immortal and possesses mystical powers (神話傳說中長生不老、有種種神通的人)". Ibid., p.682.

(8) "待" here means "rely (依靠)", as in《商君書•農戰》: "國待農戰而安, 主待農戰而尊." See《漢語大字典》. Wuhan: 崇文書局, 2010, p.879.

(9) The "yellow crane (黃鶴)" here alludes to a legend that Prince Jin (太子晉) of the Zhou Dynasty transcended to the skies by riding a crane. See 劉向,《列仙傳》Vol.1, 王子喬. 欽定四庫全書子部十二, 乾隆四十六年版, p.14b.

(10) "海客" here means "a wanderer who roams all over the world (浪跡四海者)", as in 張固《幽閑鼓吹》: "丞相牛僧孺應舉時, 知於頓相奇俊, 特詣襄陽求知. 住數日, 兩見, 以海客遇之, 牛公怒而去." See《漢語大詞典》. Shanghai: 上海辭書出版社, 2008, p.1224.

(11) "Qu Ping (屈平)" is Qu Yuan (屈原, 340 BC – 278 BC), a renowned literati and statesman during the Warring States period.

See 司馬遷《史記》Vol.84, 屈原賈生列傳. Hong Kong: 廣智書局, publication year unknown, p.47.

(12) "辭賦" here refers to the "Chu Verses (楚辭)", which is a literary form first introduced by Qu Yuan (屈原). See《漢語大詞典》. Shanghai: 上海辭書出版社, 2008, p.506.

(13) "臺榭" here means "terraces (臺) and pavilions (榭)", as in 《書•泰誓上》："惟宮室臺榭, 陂池侈服, 以殘害於爾萬姓." 孔穎達疏引李巡曰："臺, 積土爲之, 所以觀望也. 臺上有屋謂之榭." See 《漢語大詞典》. Shanghai: 上海辭書出版社, 2008, p.799.

(14) "空" here means "void (沒有)", as in 上官儀《從駕閭山詠馬》："桂香塵處減, 練影月前空." See《漢語大字典》. Wuhan: 崇文書局, 2010, p.2910.

(15) "興" here means "joy (興致)", as in《晉書•王徽之傳》："乘興而來, 興盡便返." Ibid., p.131.

(16) "酣" here means "drunk (醉)", as in 白居易《秦中吟•輕肥》："食飽心自若, 酒酣氣益振." See《漢語大詞典》. Shanghai: 上海辭書出版社, 2008, p.1396.

(17) "五嶽" here refers to the "Five Great Mountains in China (五大名山的總稱)", which may include "Mount Tai of Shandong (泰山)", "Mount Hua of Shaanxi (華山)", "Mount Song of Henan (嵩山)", "Mount Heng of Shanxi (恆山)", and "Mount Heng of Hunan (衡山)". Ibid., p.390.

(18) "笑傲" here means "contemptuous amusement (戲謔不敬)", as in《詩•邶風•終風》："謔浪笑敖, 中心是悼." 毛傳: "言戲謔不敬." Ibid., p.1110.

(19) "滄洲" here refers to "a place of reclusive delight (避世歸隱之地)". See Remarks (II).

(20) "漢水" refers to the Han River that flows southeast from to-day's Shaanxi province (陝西省) towards the Yangtze River (長江). See 酈道元《水經注》Vol.20 . Shanghai: 中華書局, 1936, pp.1-16.

(21) 郁賢皓,《李白大辭典》. Nanning: 廣西教育出版社, 1995, p.441.

(22) Ibid., p.530.

(23) 詹鍈,《李白全集校注匯釋集評》. Tianjin: 百花文藝出版社, 1996, p.993.

(24) 歐陽修,《新唐書》Vol.203, 吳融傳. Beijing: 中華書局, 1975, p.5788.

(25) 曹寅,《全唐詩》Vol.686. 欽定四庫全書薈要集部, 康熙四十六年版, p.8a.

(26) Ibid., Vol.684, p.8b.

(27) Ibid., Vol.225, p.8b.

(28) 唐圭璋,《全宋詞》Vol.3. Beijing: 中華書局, 1999, p.2065.

(29) 曹寅,《全唐詩》Vol.148. Beijing: 中華書局, 1979, p.1525.

(30) Ibid., Vol.648, p.7445.

(31) Ibid., Vol.168, p.1739.

Bai Juyi
An Inscription Regarding the Yuquan Temple

白居易
《题玉泉寺》

Calligraphy

Calligrapher (書者): KS Vincent Poon (潘君尚)

Content (內容): *An Inscription Regarding the Yuquan Temple,* a poem by Bai Juyi (白居易《題玉泉寺》)

Style (字體): Standard Script (楷書)

Caption (款識): 白居易題玉泉寺詩意頗深甲辰冬潘君尚遣閒 (Bai Juyi, *An Inscription Regarding the Yuquan Temple*, the poetic theme of which is quite profound. Year of the Jiachen, Winter, Kwan Sheung Vincent Poon scribed in leisure)

Seal Inscription (鈐印): 君尚 (朱文) (Kwan Sheung Vincent, red characters), 潘氏 (白文) (The Surname of Poon, white characters)

Medium (材料): Ink on Xuan paper (紙墨水本)

Size (尺寸): 68 X 35cm

Year (年份): 2025

湛湛玉泉色悠悠浮雲身

閒心對定水清淨兩無塵

手把青筇杖頭戴白綸巾

興盡下山去知我是誰人

白居易題玉泉寺詩意頗深甲辰冬潘君尚遣閒

Translation

白居易《題玉泉寺》
Bai Juyi, *An Inscription Regarding the Yuquan Temple*

湛湛玉泉色，悠悠浮雲身。閒心對定水，清淨兩無塵。手把青筇杖，頭戴白綸巾。興盡下山去，知我是誰人。

白話對譯 Vernacular Chinese

濃濃景色的玉泉寺，悠悠浮雲的閒適身。安閒的心，應答澄靜的水。清清淨淨，兩不染俗塵。手執青筇手杖，頭戴白綸絲巾。盡興之後下山去，管得我是什麼人！

English

1. 湛湛玉泉色 ，
The rich (湛湛)[1] Yuquan's surroundings (色)[2],

2. 悠悠浮雲身 ；
The carefree (悠悠)[3] bodies of clouds hovering;

3. 閒心對定水 ，
An easeful mind meets still waters,

4. 清淨兩無塵。
Both are tranquil, void of dusty matters.

5. 手把青筇杖 ，
My hand holding a bamboo staff (青筇杖)[4],

6. 頭戴白綸巾 ;
Head wearing a white silk scarf (白綸巾)[5];

7. 興盡下山去 ,
Overflowed with joy, off the mountain I descend,

8. 知我是誰人!
Who cares (知) who I am![6]

(translated by KS Vincent Poon, November 2024)

Remarks

(I)

An Inscription Regarding the Yuquan Temple was composed by the renowned poet Bai Juyi (白居易,772-846 AD) in 815AD[7]. That year, Bai became a casualty of a power struggle and was demoted from the capital to be the Vice Prefect of Jiangzhou (江州司馬)[8].

(II)

During that depressing time, Bai turned to Nature for enlightenment[9]. He found relief by letting go of his social identity and the public eye, as expressed in this poem. Indeed, all things in Nature do not care what others think about them. So then, why must one seek social recognition?

Footnotes

(1) "湛湛" here means "rich and intense (濃重深厚的樣子)", as in the *Book of Odes - Minor Odes of the Kingdom – Zhan Lu* (《詩經•小雅•湛露》)："湛湛露斯, 匪陽不晞." See 《漢語大詞典》Vol.5. Shanghai: 上海辭書出版社, 2008, p.1442.

(2) "色" here means "surroundings (景象)", as in *Zhuangzi - The Robber Zhi* (《莊子•盜蹠》)："車馬有行色, 得微往見蹠耶?" See 《漢語大字典》. Wuhan: 崇文書局, 2010, p.3274.

(3) "悠悠" here means "carefree (安閒暇適的樣子)", as in 高適《封丘作》："我本漁樵孟諸野, 一生自是悠悠者." See 《漢語大詞典》Vol.7. Shanghai: 上海辭書出版社, 2008, p.532.

(4) "青筇杖" refers to "a staff that is made out of Qiong bamboo". See 《漢語大字典》. Wuhan: 崇文書局, 2010, p.3150.

(5) "白綸巾" refers to "a white silk scarf" that was often worn by gentries. See 《漢語大詞典》Vol.9. Shanghai: 上海辭書出版社, 2008, pp.903-904.

(6) "知" here means "care/bother (管/理得)", as in 吳潛《八聲甘州•和魏鶴山韻》:"如何是, 一尊相屬, 萬事休知." See 《漢語大字典》. Wuhan: 崇文書局, 2010, p.2764. "誰人" here means "who (甚麼人)". See 《漢語大詞典》Vol.11. Ibid., p.285. Thus, "知我是誰人" in this poem means "who cares who I am (管我是甚麼人)".

(7) 朱金城,《白居易集箋校》. Shanghai: 上海古籍出版社, 1988, p.355.

(8) 劉昫,《舊唐書》 Vol.166, 白居易傳. Taiwan: 臺灣中華書局, 1971, pp.10-11.

(9) Ibid..

Tranquility
Ninna-ji Temple
仁和寺
Kyoto Japan

by KS Vincent Poon

Who Can I Find to Ask?
Books Kinokuniya
紀伊國屋書店
Hiroshima Japan

by KS Vincent Poon

Xue Ying
Upon the Lake on an Autumn Day

薛瑩
《秋日湖上》

Calligraphy

Calligrapher (書者): KS Vincent Poon (潘君尚)

Content (內容): *Upon the Lake on an Autumn Day,* a poem by Xue Ying (薛瑩《秋日湖上》)

Style (字體): Standard Script (楷書)

Caption (款識): 薛瑩秋日湖上甲辰潘君尚 (Xue Ying, *Upon the Lake on an Autumn Day.* Year of the Jiachen, Kwan Sheung Vincent Poon)

Seal Inscription (鈐印): 君尚 (朱文) (Kwan Sheung Vincent, red characters), 潘氏 (白文) (The Surname of Poon, white characters)

Medium (材料): Ink on Xuan paper (紙墨水本)

Size (尺寸): 72 X 36cm

Year (年份): 2024

落日五湖遊，煙波處處愁。沈浮千古事，誰與問東流。

薛瑩　秋日湖上　甲辰　潘君尚

Translation

薛瑩《秋日湖上》
Xue Ying, *Upon the Lake on an Autumn Day*

落日五湖游，煙波處處愁。沈浮千古事，誰與問東流。

白話對譯 Vernacular Chinese

日落時在五湖(洞庭湖)游玩，但見湖水煙霧蒼茫，處處哀愁。久遠前的興亡盛衰故事，唉，哪個可給我問問這些久已往東流逝的舊事呢？

English

1. 落日五湖游，
I tour the Five Lakes (五湖)[1] during Sunset,

2. 煙波處處愁。
The fog is over the surface, and everywhere seems so depressed.

3. 沈浮千古事，
The tales of the rise-and-fall (沈浮)[2] from aeons past (千古)[3],

4. 誰與問東流。
About those bygones (東流)[4], who can I find to ask?

(translated by KS Vincent Poon, November 2024)

44

Remarks

This short poem was written by Xue Ying (薛瑩) of the Tang Dynasty. Very little is known about the poet except he lived during the era of Emperor Wenzong of Tang (唐文宗, 809-840)[5], a period when the Niu–Li Factional Strife (牛李黨爭) was at its peak[6]. Many of Xue's poems are long lost[7], and only eleven of them can be found in the *Complete Tang Poems* (《全唐詩》)[8].

Footnotes

(1) "五湖" here refers to "Dongting Lake (洞庭湖)" in Hunan province (湖南省), as in 杜甫《歸雁》: "年年霜露隔, 不過五湖秋." 朱鶴齡注: "雁至衡陽則回. 此五湖當指洞庭湖言." See《漢語大詞典》. Shanghai: 上海辭書出版社, 2008, p.381.

(2) "沈浮" here is "rise and fall (盛衰) ", as in 《莊子•知北遊》: "天下莫不沈浮, 終身不故; 陰陽四時運行, 各得其序." Ibid., p.1002.

(3) "千古" here means "aeons past (久遠的年代) ", as in 酈道元《水經注•睢水四》: "追芳昔娛, 神遊千古, 故亦一時之盛事." Ibid., p.834.

(4) "東流" literally means "the waters that had already flown (流) east (東)", which is a metaphor for "bygones (事物消逝, 不可復返)", as in 李白《金陵歌送別范宣》: "四十餘帝三百秋, 功名事跡隨東流." Ibid., p.842.

(5) 陳振孫, 《直齋書錄解題》 Vol.19. 欽定四庫全書薈要史部, 乾隆四十一年版, pp.19b-20a.

(6) 司馬光,《資治通鑑》Vol.245, 胡三省注. Hong Kong: 世界書局, 1970, pp.7899-7900.

(7) 張撝之,《中國歷代人名大辭典》Vol.2. Shanghai: 上海古籍出版社, 1999, p.2536.

(8) 曹寅,《全唐詩》Vol.542. Beijing: 中華書局, 1979, pp.6264-6266.

Su Shi
Lyrics to *Nian Lu Jiao, Commemorating the Battle of Red Cliffs*

蘇軾
《念奴嬌·赤壁懷古》

Calligraphy

Calligrapher (書者): KS Vincent Poon (潘君尚)

Content (內容): Lyrics to *Nian Lu Jiao, Commemorating the Battle of Red Cliffs,* a lyrical poem by Su Shi (蘇軾《念奴嬌•赤壁懷古》)

Style (字體): Clerical Script (隸書)

Caption (款識): 蘇軾念奴嬌癸卯君尚 (Su Shi, *Nian Lu Jiao.* Year of the Guimao, Kwan Sheung Vincent)

Seal Inscription (鈐印): 君尚 (朱文) (Kwan Sheung Vincent, red characters), 潘氏 (白文) (The Surname of Poon, white characters)

Medium (材料): Ink on Xuan paper (紙墨水本)

Size (尺寸): 75 X 35cm

Year (年份): 2024

大江東去浪淘盡千古風流人物故壘西邊
人道是三國周郎赤壁亂石穿空驚濤拍岸起
千堆雪江山如畫一時多少豪傑遙想公瑾當
年小喬初嫁了雄姿英發羽扇綸巾談笑間強
虜灰飛煙滅故國神遊多情應笑我早生華髮
人間如夢一尊還酹江月

蘇軾念奴嬌 癸卯羅尚

Translation

蘇軾《念奴嬌•赤壁懷古》
Su Shi, Lyrics to *Nian Lu Jiao, Commemorating the Battle of Red Cliffs*

大江東去，浪淘盡、千古風流人物。故壘西邊，人道是、三國周郎赤壁。亂石穿空，驚濤拍岸，捲起千堆雪。江山如畫，一時多少豪傑。　遙想公瑾當年，小喬初嫁了，雄姿英發。羽扇綸巾，談笑間、強虜灰飛煙滅。故國神遊，多情應笑我、早生華髮。人間如夢，一尊還酹江月。

白話對譯 Vernacular Chinese

大江流水東奔去，浪水沖刷殆盡的、是久遠前一眾傑出人物。舊堡壘的西邊，有人說這就是、三國時周瑜(和曹操開戰) 的赤壁。江邊雜亂的石塊堆得聳若入空，震懾人心的波濤拍擊著岸邊，捲起了千堆雪般的浪花。江山美麗如畫，這時期確有很多豪傑。　遙想公瑾(周瑜)壯年，小喬剛嫁了給他，雄武才溢，神采煥發。從容自若、氣定神閒，談談笑笑之間、強暴的敵人(曹操)就給他殲個灰飛煙滅。家國神遊，對它還如此癡情的該是、這已生白髮的可笑的我。塵世如夢，倒不如帶酒一罈，敬向江上明月奠酒相對飲!

English

1. 大江東去，
The mighty River (大江) gushed to the East without turning back whatsoever,

2. 浪淘盡、千古風流人物 。
Its waves swept and expended all bygones (千古) of distinguished character (風流人物)[1].

3. 故壘西邊 ,
On the west side of the old fortress (故壘)[2],

4. 人道是、三國周郎赤壁。
Some said it was the Red Cliff (赤壁) where the Three Kingdoms'
(三國) Master Zhou (周郎, Zhou Yu) became victorious.

5. 亂石穿空 ,
The chaotic rocks at the banks erupted (穿) into the sky,

6. 驚濤拍岸 ,
Assaulting the shores were the frightening tides,

7. 捲起千堆雪。
Which rolled up thousands of snowdrifts (雪) tall and high.

8. 江山如畫 ,
The homeland (江山)[3] was as magnificent as a painting,

9. 一時多少豪傑。
Those were the days when many (多少)[4] distinguished heroes
(豪傑)[5] were living.

10. 遙想公瑾當年 ,
Remembering the distant past (遙想)[6] when Gong-jin (公瑾,
Zhou Yu) was in his prime (當年)[7],

11. 小喬初嫁了，

Lord Qiao's stunningly beautiful younger daughter (小喬) had just wedded him at that time,

12. 雄姿英發。

His bold stance (雄姿) and marvellous flair truly shined (英發).

13. 羽扇綸巾，

With composure and carefree ease[8],

14. 談笑間、強虜灰飛煙滅。

While he jested and gossiped as he pleased, all his mighty enemies (強虜)[9] turned to dust in a breeze.

15. 故國神遊，

As I wander my beloved motherland (故國)[10] in my mind,

16. 多情應笑我、早生華髮。

I laugh at myself (笑我), whose hair has already (早)[11] turned grey, for still having so much passion (多情) for it all the time.

17. 人間如夢，

Alas, the mundane realm (人間) is like an illusion (夢) in your mind,

18. 一尊還酹江月。

I might as well bring a jar of wine (一尊) to spill and drink, taking turns with the River's moon to toast each other (還酹)[12] in kind.

(translated by KS Vincent Poon, October 2024)

Remarks

(I)

This prominent lyrical poem was composed by Su Shi (蘇軾, 1037-1101)[13], one of the most representative poets of the Song Dynasty. Su's literary talent and extraordinary intellect were widely recognized at a young age[14]. Throughout his bureaucratic career, Su was known for his compassionate and effective governing, which garnered much respect from his colleagues and Emperors Renzong (仁宗) and Shenzong (神宗)[15]. However, his frank temperament and satire often offended many high officials, and so his bureaucrat life was filled with turmoils[16]. As such, revered literati Huang Tingjian (黃庭堅, 1045-1105), a peer of Su, once remarked:

"東坡文章妙天下，其短處在好罵，慎勿襲其軌也."[17]
"Su Shi's literary works are wonders amongst all under heaven, yet they had the shortcomings of him being fond of scolding others, so beware not to follow him."
(translated by KS Vincent Poon)

(II)

There are several phrases in the poem that are commonly misinterpreted. One is "羽扇綸巾", which some incorrectly interpret as a reference to Zhuge Liang (諸葛亮, 181-234). "羽扇綸巾" here certainly alludes to Zhou Yu (周瑜, 175-210), not Zhuge Liang. First, its preceding texts "周郎赤壁", "遙想公瑾" and "雄姿英發" all refer to Zhou Yu, and so it is illogical for "羽扇綸巾" to suddenly portray Zhuge Liang. Second, in various literature during and after Song, "羽扇綸巾" merely means "with composure and carefree ease (瀟灑從容)" and has nothing to do with Zhuge Liang. For instance:

I. (宋) 孝宗《賜虞允文辭免顯謨閣學士知平江府不允詔》: "<u>羽扇綸巾</u>, 嘗掃舟中之敵; 輕裘緩帶, 久宣塞上之勞."[18]

II. (宋) 謝逸《潛心堂》: "<u>羽扇綸巾</u>延客晚, 蒲團禪板坐更深."[19]

III. (元) 周巽《挽周宣慰方壺》: "<u>羽扇綸巾</u>雅量閒, 梅嶺雲歸凱初奏."[20]

IV. (元) 邵亨貞《臨江仙•擬無住水檻過雨》: "<u>羽扇綸巾</u>閑到我, 百年世事匆匆."[21]

V. (明) 沈采《千金記•登拜》: "得志也<u>羽扇綸巾</u>."[22]

Lastly and more compellingly, Song's Zhao Yifu (趙以夫, 1189-1256) explicitly used "羽扇綸巾" to characterize Zhou Yu in his 《漢宮春•次方時父元夕見寄》:

"周郎少日, 風流<u>羽扇綸巾</u>."[23]
"In the days when Master Zhou was young, he was with grace, <u>composure and carefree ease</u>."
(translated by KS Vincent Poon)

Thus, Su's "羽扇綸巾" definitely alludes to Zhao Yu, not Zhuge Liang.

(III)

Another commonly misinterpreted phrase is "故國神遊, 多情應笑我". Most incorrectly interpret "故國" as "the battlefield at the Red Cliffs during the Three Kingdoms era (三國時的赤壁戰場)", and so they erroneously conclude "多情" to be "my many lamentations toward Zhou Yu's feat in the Battle of the Red Cliffs (對赤壁之戰的無限感慨)"[24]. Alas, Su expressed great admiration for

Zhou's military and romantic successes at the beginning of the poem, so why would he lament Zhou's triumphs at the end? If the lamentations were directed at Su himself for not being as talented as Zhou, then that would be contrary to his character as a bold and proud man[25].

"故國" is key to correctly interpreting the entire phrase. "故國" here actually means "homeland (本國)", as can be seen in various classical works:

   I. (南朝) 丘遲《與陳伯之書》: "見故國之旗鼓, 感平生於疇昔."[26]

   II. (唐) 周賀《出關後寄賈島》: "故國知何處, 西風已度關."[27]

Since "故國" means "motherland", it follows "多情" in the poem should be taken as Su's "passion for the motherland". Given the historical context of the poem, such interpretations are certainly reasonable. In 1082, Su toured the Red Cliffs in July, having been released from political imprisonment and stripped of all de facto official capacity since 1079[28]. During that trip, Su was reminded of Zhou Yu's greatness in defeating Cao Cao, as narrated in Su's masterpiece *First Ode to the Red Cliffs* (《前赤壁賦》)[29]. In September 1082, Song suffered a tremendous military loss in the Battle of Yongle City (永樂城之戰) against the barbaric Xi Xia (西夏), losing more than two hundred thousand troops[30]. Su likely then composed this lyrical poem to bemoan that no one in charge was as capable as Zhou Yu to defeat the invaders. Indeed, the Song motherland (故國) was so hopeless that Su had to sarcastically laugh at (應笑) himself (我) for still having so much passion (多情) for it.

(IV)

"早生華髮" is another phrase that is often misinterpreted. Many interpreted "早" as "early" and claimed Su was laughing at his hair turning grey too early. However, little to no concrete historical evidence substantiates Su had premature grey hair. Further, even if Su indeed had premature grey hair, the bold and carefree Su would never be bothered by such a petty matter[31].

Instead of "early", "早" in this poem actually means "had already (已)", as in:

I. (宋) 秦觀 《阮郎歸·退花新綠漸團枝》:"日長早被酒禁持."[32]

II. (元) 盧摯 《沉醉東風·閑居》:"早來到竹籬茅舍人家."[33]

As discussed in (III), Su was sarcastically laughing at his passion for the motherland. He added "早生華髮" to further his sarcasm: even though his hair had already (早) turned grey, laughably, he still held passion for the Song regime.

(V)

There is one more phrase in the poem that deserves further elaboration. The concluding phrase "還酹江月" is often interpreted insufficiently as "to spill wine as an offering to the moon (把酒澆地以祭月)". In fact, "還" here carries a meaning of "還相", which means "taking turns (輪流)", as in *Book of Wei - Biography of Yang Jin* (《魏書·楊津傳》):

"洛周脫津衣服，…欲將烹之，諸賊還相諫止，遂得免害."[34]
"Lou Zhou undressed Jin … and was about to boil him, but Lou's fellow rebels took turns persuading him to stop, so Jin was ultimately

spared."
(translated by KS Vincent Poon)

Thus, taking turns to toast one another (人與人相敬酒) is known as "還酬", which can be seen in:

I. (宋) 劉辰翁《須溪集》: "有懷數友還酬一尊."[35]

II. (明) 吳寬《寄壽施煥伯七十》: "少待登堂成一笑, 手持春酒獻還酬."[36]

Similarly, "還酹" means "taking turns with the nonliving to toast each other", which can be seen in:

(i) (宋) 何夢桂《赤壁夢鶴》: "遼海千年約未寒, 一樽還酹大江干(岸)."[37]

(ii) (元) 耶律鑄《次韻閬州述事》: "為誰携斗酒 , 還酹魯公祠."[38]

"還酹" is a custom where one drinks to toast the nonliving and then spills wine onto the ground as if the nonliving toasts back. Thus, "還酹江月" is better interpreted as "to spill and drink, taking turns with the River's moon to toast each other" than simply "to spill wine as an offering to the moon".

Footnotes

(1) "風流" here means "outstanding (傑出不凡)", as in 蘇軾《與江惇禮秀才書》之一: "僕雖晚生, 猶及見君之王父也. 追思一時風流賢達, 豈可復夢見哉!" See《漢語大詞典》. Shanghai: 上海辭書出版社, 2008, pp.611-612.

(2) "故壘" here means "an old fortress from the distant past (古代的堡壘)", as in 《晉書•李矩傳》："劉聰遣從弟暢步騎三萬討矩, 屯於韓王故壘." Ibid., p.487.

(3) "江山" here means "homeland (國家的疆土)", as in 《三國志•吳志•賀劭傳》："割據江山, 拓土萬里." Ibid., pp.915-916. Some interpret "江山" as merely "the rivers and mountains near the Red Cliffs". Such is too narrow and restrictive for the succeeding phrase, "Those were the days when many great heroes were living (一時多少豪傑)".

(4) "多少" here means "many (許多)", as in 杜牧《江南春》詩: "南朝四百八十寺, 多少樓臺煙雨中." Ibid., p.1176.

(5) "豪傑" here means "distinguished persons (才能出眾的人)", as in 《管子•七法》："收天下之豪傑, 有天下之駿雄." Ibid., p.33.

(6) "遙想" here means "remembering the distant past (悠遠地回想)", as in 孫綽《遊天台山賦》："非夫遠寄冥搜, 篤信通神者, 何肯遙想而存之." Ibid., p.1144.

(7) "當年" here means "prime years (壯年)", as in 《墨子•非樂上》："將必使當年, 因其耳目之聰明, 股肱之畢強, 聲之和調, 眉之轉朴." 孫詒讓間詁："王云：'當年, 壯年也.' 當有盛壯之義." Ibid., p.1390.

(8) "羽扇綸巾" here means "with composure and carefree ease (瀟灑從容)". See Remarks (II) for further elaborations.

(9) "強虜" here means "mighty and ruthliess enemies (強暴的敵人)", as in 薛能《獻僕射相公》詩: "強虜外聞應喪膽, 平人相見盡開顏." See 《漢語大詞典》. Shanghai: 上海辭書出版社, 2008,

p.145.

(10) "故國" here means "motherland (本國)". See Remarks (III) for further elaborations.

(11) "早" here means "had already (已)". See Remarks (IV) for further elaborations.

(12) "還酹" here means "taking turns with the nonliving to toast each other (人與物或亡靈相敬酒)". See Remarks (V) for further elaborations.

(13) 唐圭璋,《全宋詞》Vol.1. Beijing: 中華書局, 1999, p.363.

(14) 脫脫,《宋史》Vol.338, 蘇軾傳. Taipei: 藝文印書館, 乾隆武英殿版, Book 5, p.4265.

(15) Ibid., pp.4265, 4274.

(16) Ibid., pp.4266-4274.

(17) 黃庭堅,《豫章黃先生文集》Vol.19. Shanghai: 上海商務印書館, 四部叢刊初編集部, 縮印沈氏藏宋本, publication year unknown, p.204.

(18) 洪适,《盤洲文集》Vol.3, 內制3. 欽定四庫全書集部, 乾隆四十六年版, p.9b.

(19) 謝逸,《溪堂集》Vol.4. 欽定四庫全書集部, 乾隆四十六年版, p.4a.

(20) 周巽,《性情集》Vol.6. 欽定四庫全書集部, 乾隆四十六年版, p.3b.

(21) 邵亨貞,《蟻術詞選》Vol.1. Publisher and publication year unknown, p.2b.

(22) 沈采,《千金記》Vol. 2, 登拜. Publisher and publication year unknown.

(23) 唐圭璋,《全宋詞》Vol.4. Beijing: 中華書局, 1999, p.3397.

(24) 王力,《古代漢語》Vol.4. Beijing: 中華書局, 2001, p.1557.

(25) Su Shi once wrote, "My brush holds thousands of words, and my mind carries tens of thousands of volumes of text; to counsel emperors to become as great as Shun and Yao, how hard can that be for me? (有筆頭千字，胸中萬卷，致君堯舜，此事何難? translated by KS Vincent Poon.)" See 唐圭璋,《全宋詞》Vol.1. Beijing: 中華書局, 1999, p.364.

(26) 蕭統,《昭明文選》Vol.43. 崇文書局, 同治八年版, p19a, publication place unknown. Also 姚思廉《梁書》Vol.20, 陳伯之傳. Beijing: 中華書局, 1973, p.315.

(27) 曹寅,《全唐詩》Vol.503. 欽定四庫全書薈要集部, 康熙四十六年版, p.11b.

(28) 蘇軾,《蘇東坡集》Vol.2, 東坡先生年譜. Changsai: 商務印書館, 1939, pp.24-26.

(29) 吳楚材,《言文對照詳細註解古文觀止》Vol.11. Shanghai: 國學研究社出版, 1949, pp.228-229.

(30) 陳邦瞻,《宋史紀事本末》Vol.9, 西夏用兵. 欽定四庫全書史部, 乾隆四十九年版, pp.19-20.

(31) As in footnote (25).

(32) 唐圭璋,《全宋詞》Vol.1. Beijing: 中華書局, 1999, p.596.

(33) 任中敏,《元曲三百首》. Chongqing: 中華書局, 1945, p.16.

(34) 魏收,《魏書》Vol.8, 楊津傳. Beijing: 中華書局, 1974, p.1299.

(35) 劉辰翁,《須溪集》Vol.7. 欽定四庫全書集部, 乾隆四十六年版, p.48b.

(36) 吳寬,《家藏集》Vol.29. 欽定四庫全書集部, 乾隆四十一年版, p.13b.

(37) 何夢桂,《潛齋集》Vol.2. 欽定四庫全書集部, 乾隆四十三年版, p.33.

(38) 耶律鑄,《雙溪醉隱集》Vol.5. 欽定四庫全書集部, 乾隆四十六年版, p.6.

Waters Naturally Flow
Ohori Park Japanese Garden
枯山水, 大濠公園日本庭園
Fukuoka Japan

by KS Vincent Poon

Li Qingzhao
Lyrics to *A Sprig of Plum Blossom, The Red Lotus Flower Withered, the Bamboo Mat Tattered*

李清照
《一剪梅·紅藕香殘玉簟秋》

Calligraphy

Calligrapher (書者): KS Vincent Poon (潘君尚)

Content (內容): Lyrics to *A Sprig of Plum Blossom, The Red Lotus Flower Withered, the Bamboo Mat Tattered,* a lyrical poem by Li Qingzhao (李清照《一剪梅•紅藕香殘玉簟秋》)

Style (字體): Cursive Script (草書)

Caption (款識): 李清照一剪梅甲辰秋月潘君尚一揮 (Li Qingzhao, *A Sprig of Plum Blossom.* Year of the Jiachen, in an Autumn month, Kwan Sheung Vincent Poon scribed flowingly with great ease and liberty)

Seal Inscription (鈐印): 君尚 (朱文) (Kwan Sheung Vincent, red characters), 潘 (白文) (Poon, white character)

Medium (材料): Ink on Xuan paper (紙墨水本)

Size (尺寸): 95 X 43cm

Year (年份): 2024

红藕香残玉簟秋
轻解罗裳独上兰舟
云中谁寄锦书来雁字回时月满
西楼花自飘零水自流一种相思两
雨处闲愁此情无计可消除才下眉头
却上心头

李清照一剪梅甲辰秋月津灵书一挥

Translation

李清照《一剪梅‧紅藕香殘玉簟秋》
Li Qingzhao, Lyrics to *A Sprig of Plum Blossom, The Red Lotus Flower Withered, the Bamboo Mat Tattered*

紅藕香殘玉簟秋，輕解羅裳，獨上蘭舟。雲中誰寄錦書來? 雁字回時，月滿西樓。　花自飄零水自流，一種相思，兩處閒愁。此情無計可消除，才下眉頭，卻上心頭。

白話對譯 Vernacular Chinese

紅蓮花謝，竹席破舊，鬆開羅衣，獨自登上小舟。(夫君在)雲中(給金石迷住了，) 哪個會寄情書來? (他日)雁群飛回時，共賞月圓於西樓。　花自凋謝，水自流動，同樣相思，兩地分隔帶來無端的情愁。這相思愁情沒法可消除，—— 剛鬆下眉頭，卻立又湧上心頭!

English

1. 紅藕香殘玉簟秋，
The red lotus (紅藕)[1] flower (香)[2] withered, the bamboo mat (玉簟)[3] tattered (秋)[4],

2. 輕解羅裳，獨上蘭舟。
Relaxing (輕解)[5] my silk outerwear, I board a small boat (蘭舟)[6] with no other.

3. 雲中誰寄錦書來?

Who (my husband) in Yunzhong (雲中, where Li's husband was obsessively looking for ancient relics of inscriptions)[7] will send me a love letter (錦書)[8]?

4. 雁字回時，月滿西樓。

When the flock of geese (雁字)[9] returns, we shall enjoy the full moon at the West Pavilion (Xi Lou, 西樓) together.

5. 花自飄零水自流，

Flowers naturally wither as the waters naturally flow,

6. 一種相思，兩處閒愁。

One mutual yearning (相思)[10], two places of inexplicable sorrow (閒愁)[11].

7. 此情無計可消除，

No way (無計) can these emotions be let go (消除),

8. 才下眉頭，卻上心頭。

Just as they retire (下) from my eyebrows, they rise (上) to reach my very soul (心頭)[12].

Remarks

(I)

Li Qingzhao (李清照, 1084 – 1151 AD) wrote this poem in 1103 AD[13], two years after her marriage to scholar and bureaucrat Zhao Mingcheng (趙明誠, 1081-1129 AD)[14]. Zhao had always been obsessed with ancient bronze and stone inscriptions (金石)[15], and Li composed this poem to express her parting sorrows when he left home in search of relics[16]. Despite this, Li played an active role in completing Zhao's masterpiece *Catalogue of Bronze and Stone Inscriptions* (《金石錄》) before his death in 1129 AD[17].

(II)

"雲中" in this poem is often misinterpreted as "the distant white clouds (遠天白雲)", which is nonsensical and too literal. Judging from the circumstances surrounding Li and her husband Zhao, "雲中" here undoubtedly refers to the Yunzhong territory (雲中府), which is renowned for its stone relics, including the landmark Yungang Grottoes (雲崗石窟)[18]. Zhao's ardent affection for ancient stone inscriptions likely led him to places like Yunzhong all by himself, and Li lamented that once Zhao was in such sites, he would completely forget about her[19]. Hence, she bemoaned, "Who in Yunzhong will send me a love letter (雲中誰寄錦書來)?" and hoped, upon his return, they could "enjoy the full moon at the West Pavilion together (月滿西樓)".

Footnotes

(1) "紅藕" here means "red lotus (紅蓮)", as in 裴說《旅次衡陽》: "晚秋紅藕裏, 十宿寄漁船." See 《漢語大詞典》. Shanghai: 上海辭書出版社, 2008, p.717.

(2) "香" here serves as "a metaphor for flower (借指花)", as in 李

賀《金銅仙人辭漢歌》: "畫欄桂樹懸秋香，三十六宮土花碧." Ibid., p.423.

(3) "玉簟" here means "bamboo mat (竹席)", as in 韋應物《馬明生遇神女歌》: "石壁千尋啓雙檢, 中有玉牀鋪玉簟." Ibid., p.518.

(4) "秋" here means "tattered (殘破/蕭條)", as in 胡曾《詠史詩•鴻溝》: "虎倦龍疲白刃秋, 兩分天下指鴻溝." Ibid., p.34.

(5) "輕解" here means "relaxing one's clothing (鬆開羅衣)", as in 張大復《梅花草堂筆談•三境》: "我醉欲眠, 鼠奔鳥竄; 羅襦輕解, 鼻息如雷. 此一境界, 亦足賞心." See 張大復《梅花草堂筆談》Vol 3. Shanghai: 上海雜誌, 1935, p.49.

(6) "蘭舟" here is "an euphemism for a small boat (小舟的美稱)", as in 許渾《重遊練湖懷舊》詩: "西風渺渺月連天, 同醉蘭舟未十年." See《漢語大詞典》. Shanghai: 上海辭書出版社, 2008, p.627.

(7) "雲中" refers to a geographical territory that is near today's Datong in the province of Shanxi (山西大同). See Remarks (II).

(8) "錦書" is "錦字書", which is "a love letter between husband and wife (夫妻的情書信)", as in 李白《久別離》: "況有錦字書, 開緘使人嗟." See《漢語大詞典》. Shanghai: 上海辭書出版社, 2008, pp.1333 and 1335.

(9) "雁字" here means "a flock of geese (成列而飛的雁群)". The term originated from 白居易《江樓晚眺景物鮮奇吟玩成篇寄水部張員外》: "風翻白浪花千片, 雁點青天字一行." Ibid., p.804.

(10) "相思" here means "mutual yearning (彼此想念)", as in 蘇武

《留別妻》: "生當復來歸, 死當長相思." Ibid., p.1147.

(11) "閒愁" here means "inexplicable sorrows (無端無謂的憂愁)", as in 張碧《惜花》: "一窖閒愁驅不去, 殷勤對爾酌金杯." Ibid., p.89.

(12) "心頭" here means "mind and soul (心間)", as in 朱淑真《秋夜聞雨》: "獨宿廣寒多少恨, 一時分付我心頭." Ibid., p.392.

(13) 徐培均, 《李清照集笺注》. Shanghai: 上海古籍出版社, 2002, p.22.

(14) 李清照,《金石錄後序》. Attached in the end of 趙明誠《金石錄》. 欽定四庫全書史部, 乾隆四十一年版, attachment pp.1-6.

(15) 趙明誠,《金石錄》, 原序. Ibid., pp.1-3.

(16) As in footnote (14).

(17) Ibid..

(18) 脫脫,《宋史》Vol.90, 地理志, "雲中府". Taipei: 藝文印書館, 乾隆武英殿版, p.1106. Also 臧勵龢《中國古今地名大辭典》, "雲中府". Taipei: 臺灣商務印書館, 1966, p.967.

(19) Li once remarked Zhao was "beyond the control of himself (不能自已)" whenever he encountered ancient relics. See footnote (14), attachment p.1b.

Li Qingzhao
Lyrics to *Immortal by the River, The Courtyard Is Profoundly Tranquil and Deep, so Tranquil and Deep*

李清照
《臨江仙·庭院深深深幾許》

Calligraphy

Calligrapher (書者): KS Vincent Poon (潘君尚)

Content (內容): Lyrics to *Immortal by the River, The Court-yard Is Profoundly Tranquil and Deep, so Tranquil and Deep,* a lyrical poem by Li Qingzhao (李清照《臨江仙•庭院深深深幾許》)

Style (字體): Clerical Script (隸書)

Caption (款識): 李清照臨江仙甲辰秋潘君尚於尚尚齋 (Li Qingzhao, *Immortal by the River.* Year of the Jiachen, Autumn, Kwan Sheung Vincent Poon scribed at The Senseis)

Seal Inscription (鈐印): 君尚 (朱文) (Kwan Sheung Vincent, red characters), 潘 (白文) (Poon, white character)

Medium (材料): Ink on Xuan paper (紙墨水本)

Size (尺寸): 85 X 47cm

Year (年份): 2024

庭院深深深幾許雲窗霧閣常扃柳
梢梅萼漸分明春歸秣陵樹人老建
康城感月吟風多少事如今老去無
成誰憐憔悴更凋零試燈無意思踏
雪沒心情

李清照臨江仙甲辰秋潘君尚於尚尚齋

Translation

李清照《臨江仙·庭院深深深幾許》
Li Qingzhao, Lyrics to *Immortal by the River, The Courtyard Is Profoundly Tranquil and Deep, so Tranquil and Deep*

庭院深深深幾許，雲窗霧閣常扃。柳梢梅萼漸分明，春歸秣陵樹，人老建康城。　感月吟風多少事，如今老去無成。誰憐憔悴更凋零，試燈無意思，踏雪沒心情。

白話對譯 Vernacular Chinese

庭院幽深多麼深，華窗高閣門常關。柳樹梢末、梅花蓓蕾漸都顯明，春天來臨，秣陵(建康)的樹活起來了，人(夫君)呢，卻已死在建康城。　受寒病重、吟讀古詩文，勾起很多(共研金石的)往事，(你)如今死去，事事無成。誰個可憐(我)容顏憔悴與衰頹？預賞花燈無興趣，踏雪賞景沒心情。

English

1. 庭院深深深幾許，

The courtyard is profoundly tranquil and deep (深深), so tranquil and deep,

2. 雲窗霧閣常扃。

For all decorated windows (雲窗)[1] are invariably shut (扃)[2] in this pavilion suite (霧閣)[3].

3. 柳梢梅萼漸分明 ,
The willow tips (柳梢)[4] and plum buds (梅萼)[5] gradually come to light,

4. 春歸秣陵樹 ,
Spring has returned (歸), and Moling's (秣陵, i.e. 建康)[6] trees have come to life,

5. 人老建康城。
Yet, this very Jiankang City (建康城)[7] is where my man (人, my husband)[8] has lost his life (老)[9].

6. 感月吟風多少事 ,
Coming down with a cold (感月)[10] while chanting poems (吟風)[11], many memories (事) of you naturally arise,

7. 如今老去無成。
Yet, now you have passed away (老)[12] with no accomplishment realized.

8. 誰憐憔悴更凋零?!
Who pities me, emaciated (憔悴)[13] and (更)[14] devitalized (凋零)[15]?!

9. 試燈無意思 ,
A trip to preview the Lantern Festival (試燈)[16] serves no meaning,

10. 踏雪沒心情。
And I find no mood to walk in the snow (踏雪)[17] to go sightseeing.

Remarks

(I)

Song Dynasty female poet Li Qingzhao (李清照, 1084-1155 AD) wrote this lyrical poem in the Spring of 1130 AD[18] to mourn the death of her beloved husband Zhao Mingcheng (趙明誠, 1081-1129 AD), the author of *Catalogue of Bronze and Stone Inscriptions* (《金石錄》)[19].

In 1129, Li fled Jiankang (建康, now Nanjing, 南京) in March from the northern invading Jin (金)[20], while her husband died in August of illness[21]. Undoubtedly, 1129 was a tragic year for Li.

(II)

Several key areas in the poem are often misinterpreted.

The first is "人老建康城". Many contend it means "Li was expecting herself to turn old and perish in the city of Jiankang (看來要老死建康城)"[22]. Such is nonsensical, for Li was only 46 when she wrote this poem and no longer resided in Jiankang up to her death at 71[23].

Instead, "人" here refers to Li's husband, while "老" is a common metaphor for "death/pass away (死/逝)" in classical Chinese literature, as in:

(i) 李賀 《牡丹種曲》 : "梁王(花)老去羅衣(葉)在, 拂袖風吹蜀國弦."[24]

(ii) 子蘭 《城上吟》 : "古塚密於草, 新墳侵官道. 城外無閒地, 城中人又老."[25]

(iii) 譚用之《途中》: "光陰老去無成事, 富貴不來爭奈何."[26]
"Time has passed away, and I have accomplished nothing; wealth
has not arrived, and I can do nothing about it."
(translated by KS Vincent Poon)

Hence, "人老建康城" undoubtedly describes Li's husband's (人) death (老) in the city of Jiankang (建康城). As such, this poem was definitely composed after his burial in late 1129, during the Spring of 1130[27].

(III)

The second is "感月" in "感月吟風多少事". Many suggested "感月" here means "appreciating the moon (弄月)"[28], which is incorrect.

According to Li's own narrative in the *Epilogue of the Catalogue of Bronze and Stone Inscriptions* (《金石錄後序》), Li became exceedingly ill shortly after her husband's burial:

"葬畢, 余無所之…余有大病, 僅存喘息."[29]
"After I buried my husband, I did not know where to go…I was ex-
tremely sick and could only gasp to breathe."
(translated by KS Vincent Poon)

Hence, Li's "感月" actually means "coming down with a heavy cold (受寒病重)". Such usage can be seen in:

(i) 何休《春秋公羊傳注疏》:
"言朝者, 緣生以事死. 親在, 朝朝莫夕. 巳死, 不敢渫鬼神, 故事必於朔者. 感月始生而朝."[30]
"The so-called 'Visiting to Pay Great Respect to One's Parents (朝)'[31]
is to follow (緣) the rites of respectfully serving (事) one's living parents
when they are dead. If one's parents are alive (在), one should visit
them to pay great respect (朝) every morning (朝) and meet them to
pay high regard (夕)[32] every evening (莫). If they are no longer alive,

since one should not defile (褻) the spirits, one can respectfully serve (事) them only on the first day (朔) of the month. If one <u>comes down with a cold</u> (i.e. falls ill), one can then start (始) to visit them to pay great respect as if they were alive (生). "
(translated by KS Vincent Poon)

(ii) 白居易《感月悲逝者》:"存亡感月一潸然, 月色今宵似往年."[33]

(iii) 陳建《皇明從信錄》正德十六年 (1521 AD) 張岳上疏曰:
"近日聖躬偶感風疾, ...偶爾感月, 豈足過慮."[34]
"Recently, the Emperor occasionally came down with a cold … For one to <u>come down with a cold</u> every now and then, there is no need to be overly concerned about it. "
(translated by KS Vincent Poon)

"感" in "感月" literally means "coming down with (感染)", while "月" means "adversity and chills (陰寒)". Hence, "感月" together means "coming down with adversity and chills" or simply "falling ill".

(IV)

The third is "吟風" in "感月吟風多少事". The common interpretation is that it means "composing poems (作詩)"[35], which is incorrect. "吟風" here actually means "reviewing and chanting (吟) classical texts (風)", as supported by Li's own writing:

"寫本李、杜、韓、柳集...搬在臥內... 偶病中把玩. "[36]
"Our handwritten copies of Li's, Du's, Han's, and Liu's works ... I moved them to my bedroom...and when I was sick, I held onto and savoured them every now and then. "
(translated by KS Vincent Poon)

Hence, "感月吟風多少事" undoubtedly describes the very ill (感月) Li was reviewing and chanting (吟) the classical texts (風) compiled by her and her late husband[37], which then stirred up her many memories of him (多少事).

(V)

The final is "老" in "如今老去無成". "老" here means "death", similar to the "老" in "人老建康城" as outlined in Remarks (II). As Li recalled memories of her talented late husband (多少事), she lamented he died too early without accomplishing anything significant (老去無成).

Footnotes

(1) "雲窗" here means a "a decorated window (華美的窗戶)", as in 周邦彥《齊天樂•秋思》："暮雨生寒, 鳴蛩勤織, 深閣時聞裁剪. 雲窗靜掩." See《漢語大詞典》. Shanghai: 上海辭書出版社, 2008, p.652.

(2) "扃" here means "shut (關閉)", as in 韓愈《喜雪獻裴尚書》："履弊行偏冷, 門扃臥更羸." Ibid., p.363.

(3) "霧閣" here means "a pavilion that is covered in mist and clouds (雲霧籠罩的樓閣)", as in 高啟《仙山樓觀圖》："霧閣宵閒脈望飛, 月明露重濕銖衣." Ibid., p.728.

(4) "柳梢" here means "tips of willows (柳樹的末端)", as in 歐陽修《生查子》："月到柳梢頭, 人約黃昏後." Ibid., p.927.

(5) "梅蕚" here means "buds of plum flowers (梅花的蓓蕾)", as in 歐陽修《玉樓春•題上林後亭》："池塘隱隱驚雷曉,柳眼未開梅蕚小." Ibid., p.1049.

(6) "秣陵" refers to Jianking City (建康城), which is today's Nan-

jing (南京). See《重編國語辭典修訂本》(*Revised Mandarin Chinese Dictionary*). Taiwan: Ministry of Education, R.O.C, 2021, online edition.

(7) Ibid..

(8) "人" here refers to Li's husband. See Remarks (II) for more elaboration.

(9) "老" here means "death/pass away (死/逝)". See Remarks (II) for more elaboration.

(10) "感月" here means "coming down with a cold (受寒病重)". See Remarks (III) for more elaboration.

(11) "吟風" here means "chanting (吟) classical texts (風)". See Remarks (IV) for more elaboration.

(12) As in footnote (9).

(13) "憔悴" here means "emaciated (瘦損)", as in 王建《調笑令》: "玉顏憔悴三年, 誰復商量管絃?" See《漢語大詞典》. Shanghai: 上海辭書出版社, 2008, p.738.

(14) "更" here means "and (和)", as in 皇甫冉《雜言月洲歌送趙冽還襄陽》 : "流聒聒兮湍與瀨, 草青青兮春更秋." Ibid., p.527.

(15) "凋零" here means "devitalized (衰敗)", as in 羅隱《送汝州李中丞十二韻》: "一兇雖剪滅, 數縣尚凋零." Ibid., p.430.

(16) "試燈" refers to previewing the lanterns before the traditional Lantern Festival (元宵節), which occurs on the fifteenth day of the first month of the year (舊俗農曆正月十五日元宵節晚上張燈, 以祈豐稔, 未到元宵節而張燈預賞謂之試燈). Ibid., p.141.

(17) "踏雪" here means "to walk on the snow (在雪地行走)", as in 孟郊 《寒溪》 詩: "曉飲一杯酒, 踏雪過青溪." Ibid., p.504.

(18) Some argue "春歸秣陵樹" indicates the poem was likely composed in February of 1129 as the city of Jiankang (建康) was still named Moling (秣陵) until May of that year. This argument is flawed because Jiankang also appears in the poem, which means the poem must have been composed after May of 1129, when Li had already fled Jiankang.

Li wrote this phrase to merely contrast Jiankang's ever-returning Spring with her never-returning late husband, who died in that very city (人老建康城). Thus, "秣陵" alone is insufficient to conclude when and where the poem was actually composed.

Most reasonably, "春歸秣陵樹, 人老建康城" was written in the Spring of 1130, several months after Li's husband's burial, when she particularly missed her late husband while Nature was lively and rejuvenated. See Remark (II) for further elaboration.

(19) 李清照, 《金石錄後序》. Attached in the end of 趙明誠 《金石錄》. 欽定四庫全書史部, 乾隆四十一年版, pp.1-6.

(20) Ibid..

(21) Ibid..

(22) 趙曉輝, 《李清照》. Beijing: 五洲傳播出版社, 2005, p.107.

(23) 徐培均, 《李清照集箋注》. Shanghai: 上海古籍出版社, 2002, pp.470-512. Also, see footnote (18).

(24) 曹寅, 《全唐詩》 Vol.392. Beijing: 中華書局, 1979, p.4419.

(25) Ibid., Vol.824, p.9288.

(26) Ibid., Vol.764, p.8674.

(27) As in footnote (18).

(28) As in footnote (22).

(29) As in footnote (19).

(30) 何休,《春秋公羊傳注疏》Vol.13. 欽定四庫全書經部, 乾隆四十年版, p.20.

(31) "朝" here means "to visit and pay great respect to one's elderly parents (問候長輩)", as in 《國語•魯語下》 : "(公父文伯)朝其母, 其母方績." See《漢語大詞典》. Shanghai: 上海辭書出版社, 2008, p.1310.

(32) "夕" here means "to visit and pay great respect to one's elderly parents in the evening (傍晚拜見尊長)", as in 《左傳•成公九年》: "其爲大子也, 師保奉之, 以朝於嬰齊而夕於側也." 杜預注: "言其尊卿敬老." Ibid., p.1146.

(33) As in footnote (24), Vol.436, p.4838.

(34) 陳建,《皇明從信錄》Vol. 27. 萬曆四十八年沈國元訂, Book 9. Publication place and year unknown, p.32.

(35) As in footnote (22).

(36) As in footnote (19).

(37) Ibid..

Li Qingzhao
Lyrics to *Wulin Chun, Late Spring*

李清照
《武陵春·春晚》

Calligraphy

Calligrapher (書者): KS Vincent Poon (潘君尚)

Content (內容): Lyrics to *Wulin Chun, Late Spring,* a lyrical poem by Li Qingzhao (李清照《武陵春•春晚》)

Style (字體): Clerical Script (隸書)

Caption (款識): 李清照武陵春癸卯潘君尚 (Li Qingzhao, *Wulin Chun.* Year of the Guimao, Kwan Sheung Vincent Poon)

Seal Inscription (鈐印): 君尚 (朱文) (Kwan Sheung Vincent, red characters), 潘氏 (白文) (The Surname of Poon, white characters)

Medium (材料): Ink on Xuan paper (紙墨水本)

Size (尺寸): 67 X 44cm

Year (年份): 2023

風住塵香華已盡，日晚倦梳頭。物是人非事二休，欲語淚先流。聞說雙溪春尚好，也擬泛輕舟。只恐雙溪舴艋舟，載不動許多愁。

李清照　武陵春　癸卯書於玉香堂

Translation

李清照《武陵春·春晚》
Li Qingzhao, Lyrics to *Wulin Chun, Late Spring*

風住塵香花已盡，日晚倦梳頭。物是人非事事休，欲語淚先流。聞說雙溪春尚好，也擬泛輕舟。只恐雙溪舴艋舟，載不動許多愁。

白話對譯 Vernacular Chinese

春風已息、微香殘留，花開已到了盡頭，日晝將盡，還是懶得去梳妝。景物依舊、人面全非，事事都罷休，正欲訴說，眼淚卻已先流。　聽説雙溪春色仍然好，也打算往那裡泛小舟。只恐怕雙溪舴艋細小舟，載的是它浮不動的許多(沈重的)哀愁。

English

1. 風住塵香花已盡，
The spring wind retired (風住), only a light hint of floral fragrance (塵香)[1] lingered, and flowers had long exhausted their blooms,

2. 日晚倦梳頭。
Even late in the day (日晚)[2], I was fed up (倦)[3] with combing my head to groom.

3. 物是人非事事休，
The scenery remained (物是)[4], but the people did not (人非)[5], and every affair (事事)[6] had come to a hopeless end (休),

4. 欲語淚先流。
As I tried to find words, tears had already flowed without my command.

5. 聞說雙溪春尚好，
I heard the Twin Streams (雙溪)[7] was still full of fantastic Spring scenery,

6. 也擬泛輕舟。
And I should prepare (擬)[8] to drift (泛) on a light boat to see all the beauty.

7. 只恐雙溪舴艋舟，
Yet, I feared this tiny boat (舴艋舟)[9] on the Twin Streams was too small,

8. 載不動許多愁。
It could only withstand (載)[10] but not sway (動)[11] that much sorrow at all.

Remarks

(I)

This lyrical poem was composed by Li Qingzhao (李清照, 1084 – 1151 AD), one of the greatest poets in Chinese history[12]. It was written in 1135 AD when the Song Dynasty faced an aggressive invasion by Jin (金)[13]. At that time, Li was fleeing Lin'an (臨安) to Jinhua (金華)[14].

(II)

Li was born into an aristocratic family. Her father, Li Gefei (李格非, 1045-1105 AD), was a renowned literati[15] and a revered government official[16]. Her mother was also adept at writing[17]. At a very young age, Li married Zhao Mingcheng (趙明誠, 1081-1129 AD), who was a scholar[18] and the son of senior statesman Zhao Tingzhi (趙挺之, 1040-1107 AD)[19]. After marriage, Li helped Zhao Mingcheng finish his masterpiece *Catalogue of Bronze and Stone Inscriptions* (《金石錄》) before his death in 1129 AD[20]. This poem was composed six years after Zhao's death.

(III)

There are several phrases in this poem that are commonly misinterpreted. First, "塵香" is typically interpreted as "the soil carrying floral fragrance (塵土裡帶有花的香氣)". This sort of interpretation is incorrect. "塵" here does not refer to "soil (土)". Rather, "塵" here is the adjective "a light hint of (塵輕)" for the noun "fragrance (香)". Such usage can be seen in various classical literary works of the Song, Yuan and Ming Dynasties:

I. (宋) 蘇軾 《元夕夜游絕句》: "午夜朧朧淡月黃, 夢回猶有暗塵香."[21]

II. (宋) 吳文英 《木蘭花慢•餞韓似齋赴江東餱幕》: "潤寒梅細雨, 卷燈火、暗塵香."[22]

III. (元) 宋无 《春愁》: "金雁(箏柱)塵香暗鳳絃, 紅繩風緊閣秋千."[23]

IV. (明) 楊慎 《望西山》 : "行行國艷皆桃李, 處處塵香盡綺羅."[24]

In all four instances above, "塵" cannot take the meaning of "soil".

Thus, "塵香" should be "a light hint of floral fragrance."

(IV)

Another commonly misinterpreted phrase is "物是人非". Many, like Ming Dynasty's Ye Sheng (葉盛, 1420-1474 AD)[25] and Zhang Yan (張綖, 1487-1543 AD)[26], took "物是人非" as something like "My late husband's things are still here, but he no longer lives". Using this, they even accused Li of being immoral, for she openly expressed a longing for her late husband while married to a new one[27]. Such is utterly absurd. First, Li's remarriage is highly dubious as it is based on one unverifiable document and is contrary to Li's everlasting love for Zhao Mingcheng. Second, Li was merely borrowing Cao Pi's (曹丕, 187-226 AD) words to lament the fall of her motherland while fleeing Lin'an:

"節同時異，物是人非."[28]
"The seasons are the same, yet the times have changed; the scenery remained, but the people did not."
(translated by KS Vincent Poon)

It is reasonable for Li to display such patriotic lamentation, for she had always been very passionate about her motherland, as can be seen in her earlier masterpiece, *A Quatrain Written in a Summer* (《夏日絕句》)[29]:

"生當作人傑,
死亦爲鬼雄.
至今思項羽,
不肯過江東."
"Live to be a person with gallant valour,
Die to become a ghost with a heroic aura.
Even now, we all remember Xiang Yu, the conqueror,
For he willed not to retreat East by crossing the Wu River."
(translated by KS Vincent Poon)

Thus, judging from the historical context and Li's temperament, Li's "物是人非" had little to do with her late husband. No wonder contemporary scholar Cao Shuming (曹樹銘) denounced Ye Sheng's and Zhang Yan's conjectures as "absolutely ridiculous (荒謬萬分)"[30].

Footnotes

(1) "塵" here means "a tiny amount/a light hint of a certain object (常喻事物的微小)", as in 聶夷中《古興》: "片玉一塵輕, 粒粟山丘重." See《漢語大字典》, Wuhan: 湖北四川長江出版集團, 2010, p. 517. Also, see Remarks (III) for further elaborations.

(2) "晚" here means "late in a period of time (一個時期的後一段)", as in《古詩十九首•行行重行行》: "思君令人老, 歲月忽已晚." See《漢語大詞典》. Shanghai: 上海辭書出版社, 2008, p.743.

(3) "倦" here means "fed up (厭煩)", as in《易•繫辭下》: "通其變, 使民不倦." Ibid., p.1518.

(4) "物是人非" here means "the scenery remained, but the people and circumstances did not (景物依然, 人事已非)", as in 曹丕《與吳質書》: "節同時異, 物是人非, 我勞如何!" Ibid., p.253. Also, see Remarks (IV) for further elaborations.

(5) Ibid..

(6) "事事" here mean "Each and every affair (每事)", as in《書•說命中》: "惟事事乃其有備, 有備無患." 孔傳: "事事, 非一事." Ibid., p.548.

(7) "雙溪" here refers to the Twin Streams in the south of Jinhua (金華), the city where Li fled to. See 徐培均,《李清照集笺注》. Shanghai: 上海古籍出版社, 2002, p.142.

(8) "擬" here means "prepare (準備)", as in 柳永《鳳棲梧》詞： "擬把疏狂圖一醉, 對酒當歌, 強樂還無味." See《漢語大詞典》. Shanghai: 上海辭書出版社, 2008, p.936.

(9) "舴艋" refers to a "small boat (小舟)", as indicated in《玉篇》： "舴艋, 小舟也." Ibid., p.6.

(10) "載" here means "withstand (承受)", as in《三國志•魏志•王基傳》: "臣聞古人以水喻民, 曰'水所以載舟, 亦所以覆舟'." Ibid., p.1242.

(11) "動" here means "sway (搖)", as in《庾信•夢入內堂詩》: "日光釵焰動, 窗影鏡花搖." See《康熙字典》. Shanghai: 上海書店, 1985, p.155.

(12) 鄭振鐸,《中國文學史》. Shanghai: 上海商務印館, 1932, p.505.

(13) 徐培均, as in footnote (7), p.141.

(14) Ibid..

(15) As in footnote (12).

(16) 脫脫,《宋史》Vol.444, 李格非傳. Taipei: 藝文印書館, 乾隆武英殿版, Book 7, pp.5390-5391.

(17) 鄭振鐸, as in footnote (12), p.506.

(18) Ibid..

(19) 《宋史》, as in footnote (16), p.5391.

(20) 趙明誠,《金石錄》, *Li Qingzhao's Epilogue*《金石錄後序》. 欽定四庫全書史部, 乾隆四十一年版, pp.1-6.

(21) 蘇軾,《東坡全集》Vol.28. 欽定四庫全書集部, 乾隆四十六年版, p.21a.

(22) 唐圭璋,《全宋詞》Vol.4. Beijing: 中華書局, 1999, p.3697.

(23) 顧嗣立,《元詩選》Vol.21. 秀野草堂, publication place and year unknown, p.5a.

(24) 楊慎,《升菴集》Vol.39. 欽定四庫全書集部, 乾隆四十三年版, p.1b.

(25) 葉盛,《水東日記》Vol.21. 欽定四庫全書子部, 乾隆四十三年版, p.12.

(26) 徐培均, as in footnote (7), p.143.

(27) As in footnotes (25)&(26).

(28) 曹丕,《與朝歌令吳質書》. See《藝文類聚》compiled by 歐陽詢, Vol. 26. 欽定四庫全書子部, 乾隆四十四年版, p 28a.

(29) KS Vincent Poon, *Calligraphy Meets Philosophy - Talk 3*. Toronto: The Senseis, 2024, p.38.

(30) 曹樹銘,《李清照詩詞文存》. Taipei: 臺灣商務印書館, 1992, p.105.

Li Qingzhao
An Inscription Regarding the Ba Yong House

李清照
《題八詠樓》

Calligraphy

Calligrapher (書者): KS Vincent Poon (潘君尚)

Content (內容): A phrase from *An Inscription Regarding the Ba Yong House,* a poem by Li Qingzhao (李清照《八詠樓》句)

Style (字體): Cursive Script (草書)

Caption (款識): 李清照題八詠樓句癸卯潘君尚 (Li Qingzhao, a phrase from *An Inscription Regarding the Ba Yong House.* Year of the Guimao, Kwan Sheung Vincent Poon)

Seal Inscription (鈐印): 君尚 (朱文) (Kwan Sheung Vincent, red characters), 潘 (白文) (Poon, white character)

Medium (材料): Ink on Xuan paper (紙墨水本)

Size (尺寸): 67 X 42cm

Year (年份): 2023

千古風流八詠樓江山留與後人愁

李清照題八詠樓句癸卯泮夹書

Translation

李清照《題八詠樓》
Li Qingzhao, *An Inscription Regarding the Ba Yong House*

千古風流八詠樓，江山留與後人愁。水通南國三千里，氣壓江城十四州。

白話對譯 Vernacular Chinese

久遠前的灑脫放逸，餘韻在這八詠樓; 家國大事，就留給後人去憂愁。(樓建婺江旁) 水道通達江南幾千里，景象冠壓江浙(吳越十四州)沿江城。

English

1. 千古風流八詠樓，
Aeons (千古)[1] of carefree elegance (風流)[2] lingers at the Ba Yong House (八詠樓)[3],

2. 江山留與後人愁。
Let's leave the motherland (江山)[4] to our descendants (後人)[5] to grieve about.

3. 水通南國三千里，
Its grand waterway (水) traverses (通) the southern territories (南國)[6] for thousands (三千)[7] of lis (里)[8],

4. 氣壓江城十四州。
The surrounding scenery (氣)[9] surpasses (壓)[10] all the Fourteen Prefectures' (十四州)[11] river cities (江城)[12].

Remarks

This poem was composed by Li Qingzhao (李清照, 1084 – 1151 AD). It was written in 1135 AD when the Song Dynasty faced an aggressive invasion by Jin (金)[13]. During that same year, Li also wrote her masterpiece, *Lyrics to Wulin Chun, Late Spring* (《武陵春•春晚》), while fleeing Lin'an (臨安) to Jinhua (金華)[14].

Footnotes

(1) "千古" here means "aeons past (久遠的年代)", as in 酈道元 《水經注•睢水四》:"追芳昔娛, 神遊千古, 故亦一時之盛事." See 《漢語大詞典》. Shanghai: 上海辭書出版社, 2008, p.834.

(2) "風流" here means "carefree elegance (灑脫放逸, 風雅瀟灑)", as in 牟融《送友人》 :"衣冠重文物, 詩酒足風流." Ibid., p.611.

(3) The renowned "Ba Yong House (八詠樓)" was constructed in 494 AD at today's Jinhua (金華) in the province of Zhejiang (浙江省). Ibid., p.17.

(4) "江山" here means "motherland (國家的疆土)", as in 《三國志•吳志•賀劭傳》:"割據江山, 拓土萬里." Ibid., pp.915-916.

(5) "後人" here means "descendants (子孫/後裔)", as in 《書•太甲上》:"旁求俊彥, 啟迪後人." Ibid., p.956.

(6) "南國" here means "the southern territories (國之南方)", as in 《楚辭•九章•橘頌》 :"受命不遷, 生南國兮. " 王逸注: "南國, 謂江南也." Ibid., p.898.

(7) "三" here means "屢次(many or multiple times)" like in "三思". See 《重編國語辭典修訂本》(*Revised Mandarin Chinese Dictionary*). Taiwan: Ministry of Education, R.O.C, 2021, online edition. Thus, "三千" here means "many thousands", not "three thousand".

(8) "Li (里)" is a unit measure of distance, which is approximately three hundred or three hundred sixty footsteps. See《漢語大字典》. Wuhan: 崇文書局, 2010, p.3923.

(9) "氣" here means "sceneries (景象)", as in 杜甫《秋興》: "玉露凋傷楓樹林, 巫山巫峽氣蕭森." Ibid., p.2157.

(10) "壓" here means "surpass (超越)", as in 柳宗元《與蕭翰林俛書》 : "才不能踰同列, 聲不能壓當世." See《漢語大詞典》. Shanghai: 上海辭書出版社, 2008, p.1232.

(11) "十四州" refers to the "Fourteen Prefectures of Wuyue (吳越十四州)" occupied by Qian Liu (錢鏐, 852-932 AD) during the later years of the Tang Dynasty. See 尤袤《全唐詩話》Vol.6. Published by 伊蔚堂, year and place unknown, pp.36-37. Geographically, "十四州" is now the entire province of Zhejiang (浙江全省), the southeastern part of Jiangsu (江蘇東南部) and the northeastern part of Fujian (福建東北部). See 張傳璽, 《中國古代史教學參考地圖集》. Beijing: 北京大學出版社, 1984, p.39.

(12) "江城" here means "cities beside large rivers (臨江之城市)", as in 崔湜《襄陽早秋寄岑侍郎》: "江城秋氣早, 旭且坐南闈." See《漢語大詞典》. Shanghai: 上海辭書出版社, 2008, p.919.

(13) 徐培均, 《李清照集箋注》. Shanghai: 上海古籍出版社, 2002, pp.141, 241-242.

(14) Ibid..

Lu You
Lyrics to *Professing My Innermost Passion, In My Prime, I Cast My Aspiration Far and Wide to Seek Titles of Military Glory*

陸游
《訴衷情·當年萬里覓封侯》

Calligraphy

Calligrapher (書者): KS Vincent Poon (潘君尚)

Content (內容): Lyrics to *Professing My Innermost Passion, In My Prime, I Cast My Aspiration Far and Wide to Seek Titles of Military Glory,* a lyrical poem by Lu You (陸游《訴衷情•當年萬里覓封侯》)

Style (字體): Cursive Script (草書)

Caption (款識): 陸游訴衷情甲辰潘君尚一揮 (Lu You, *Professing My Innermost Passion.* Year of the Jiachen, Kwan Sheung Vincent Poon scribed flowingly with great ease and liberty)

Seal Inscription (鈐印): 潘 (朱文) (Poon, red character), 君尚 (白文) (Kwan Sheung Vincent, white characters)

Medium (材料): Ink on Xuan paper (紙墨水本)

Size (尺寸): 102 X 55cm

Year (年份): 2024

當年萬里覓封侯，匹馬戍梁州。關河夢斷何處，塵暗舊貂裘。胡未滅，鬢先秋，淚空流。此生誰料，心在天山，身老滄洲。

陸游訴衷情甲辰潘君書一揮

Translation

陸游《訴衷情•當年萬里覓封侯 》
Lu You, Lyrics to *Professing My Innermost Passion, In My Prime, I Cast My Aspiration Far and Wide to Seek Titles of Military Glory*

當年萬里覓封侯，匹馬戍梁州。關河夢斷何處？塵暗舊貂裘。 胡未滅，鬢先秋，淚空流。此生誰料，心在天山，身老滄洲!

白話對譯 Vernacular Chinese

壯時志向萬里遠，覓取軍功獲封侯，(很想)單人匹馬前去戍守要地梁州。如今收復關中的夢醒了，此刻關中在哪？僅剩得一件滿佈塵埃、黯然無光的舊貂裘。 胡人還未消滅，顏鬢卻先衰老，淚是白流的了。怎料此生，心在抗胡的天山，身卻死在歸隱的地方!

English

1. 當年萬里覓封侯，
In my prime (當年)[1], I cast my aspiration far and wide (萬里)[2] to seek (覓封) titles of military glory (侯).

2. 匹馬戍梁州。
Alas, how I longed to defend (戍)[3] Langzhou (梁州)[4] single-handedly (匹馬)[5].

3. 關河夢斷何處，
Awakened from the dream (夢斷)[6] of retaking Guanhe (關河)[7], where is it now, actually?

4. 塵暗舊貂裘。

What's left is only my old fur coat (貂裘)[8], all dull (暗) and dusty (塵).

5. 胡未滅，

The barbarians (胡) have yet to be wiped out completely,

6. 鬢先秋，

But my sideburns (鬢)[9] have first become weary (秋),

7. 淚空流。

Tears have all been shed in vain (空), undoubtedly.

8. 此生誰料，

O, I never imagined (誰料) my entire life story,

9. 心在天山，

Was to fight at the Khangai Mountains (天山)[10] in the mind (心) only,

10. 身老滄洲!

Leaving my body (身) to perish (老)[11] in a place of reclusion seclusively (滄洲)[12]!

Remarks

(I)

This poem was composed by Song Dynasty's Lu You (陸游, 1125-1210 AD). During his time, Song faced an existential threat from the invading Jin (金)[13]. As a "patriotic" Confucian, Lu desired to be at the forefront to defeat the invaders[14]. Yet, despite his passion, he was only appointed to various clerical advisory positions and had never commanded an army nor even fought on the front lines[15].

(II)

There are several phrases in this poem that are commonly misinterpreted.

First is "當年萬里覓封侯". Many took "當年" as "recalling those years (回憶當年)" and so contended Lu was looking back on his time as a soldier fighting the invaders (回憶早年慷慨從戎的戰鬥生活)[16]. Such is incorrect, for Lu was never a combatant on the battlefield fighting the Jins (金人), according to official records[17]. At most, he was a mere "clerical assistant officer (幹辦公事)" who once advised Military Commissioner Wang Yan (王炎) in Langzhou (梁州)[18].

Since Lu was never a soldier, "當年萬里覓封侯" has nothing to do with Lu's "combat military life". Instead, it only characterizes Lu's far and wide (萬里) aspirations to seek (覓封) titles of military glory (侯) when he was in his prime (當年). Examining various classical Chinese literature, "當年" often represented "prime (壯年)", for instance:

(i) 呂不韋《呂氏春秋•愛類》："士有當年而不耕者, 則天下或受其饑矣."[19]

(ii) 墨子《墨子•非樂上》："將必使當年, 因其耳目之聰明, 股肱之畢強, 聲之和調, 眉之轉朴."[20]

Similarly, "匹馬戍梁州" does not mean Lu had actually defended Langzhou as a soldier in his past. It merely portrays young Lu's fantasy of defending against the enemy at Langzhou, a critical military stronghold.

(III)

The second is "關河夢斷何處". Due to the common misconception that Lu had once battled the Jins, many interpret this phrase as something like "my time in the military defending the frontiers can now only be found in my dreams, and once awake, I don't know where I am (如今防守邊疆要塞的從軍生活只能在夢中出現，夢醒後不知身在何處)"[21]. Such is certainly nonsensical and wholly incorrect.

Lu actually wrote "關河夢斷何處" to express his anguish that Song failed to realize his dream (夢) of retaking Guanhe (關河), a vital strategic region in Chinese history. "關" here represents the Hangu Pass (函谷關) or the Tong Pass (潼關), while "河" represents the Yellow River (黃河) or the Wei River (渭水). Thus, Guanhe refers to Chang'an (長安) and its surrounding areas, which were also collectively known as "Guanzhong (關中)". Such is supported by the canonical *Records of the Grand Historian* (《史記》):

> "秦四塞之國，被山帶渭，東有關河，西有漢中."[22]
> "Qin was a secured state in all directions. It had tall mountains and great rivers. To the East, it held the Guanhe region. To the West, it possessed the Hanzhong area."
> (translated by KS Vincent Poon)

Since the Guanhe region, centred by Chang'an (長安), was vital to liberate the Central Plains (中原), Lu long advocated to reclaim it first:

> "以為經略中原必自長安始."[23]
> "(Lu) believed that if one plans to liberate the Central Plains, one

must begin with Chang'an."
(translated by KS Vincent Poon)

Such is why Lu put "defend Langzhou (戍梁州)" in the poem, as taking back Guanhe required first securing Langzhou, a critical military base southwest of Guanhe.

Of course, the declining Song never entirely took back the Guanhe region from the Jins. Thus, Lu lamented, "Awakened from the dream (夢斷) of retaking Guanhe (關河), where is it now, actually (何處)?"

(IV)

Third, "老" in "身老滄洲" means "death/pass away", while "滄洲" means "a place of seclusion". For elaborations on "老", please see *Lyrics to the Immortal by the River* (《 臨江仙 • 庭院深深深幾 許 》); for "滄洲", please see *A Chanted Poem Upon a River* (《 江上吟 》) in this book.

To conclude, Lu You was undoubtedly a good poet who wrote with powerful language, but his achievements as a public servant were nearly nonexistent. After retirement, he became a lackey of the scheming minister Han Tuozhou (韓侂胄, 1152-1207 AD)[24]. Revered Confucian scholar Zhu Xi (朱熹, 1130-1200 AD), a peer of Lu, once predicted:

"其能太高，跡太近，恐為有力者所牽挽，不得全其晚節."[25]
"His (Lu's) talents are extraordinarily high, but his bureaucratic ac-complishments (跡)[26] are too mediocre (太近)[27]. Thus, he is easily manipulated by those in power, so I am afraid he will be unable to preserve his integrity (節) late in his life."
(translated by KS Vincent Poon)

Toqto'a (脫脫, 1314-1356 AD), in his *History of Song - Biography of Lu You* (《宋史•陸游傳》), applauded Zhu for having such sharp "foresight (先見)"[28] long before Lu kowtowed to Han Tuozhou. Indeed, even renowned philosopher and historian Gu Yanwu (顧炎武, 1613-1682 AD) also admonished Li Zide (李子德, 1631-1692 AD) never to follow in Lu's footsteps during the early Qing Dynasty[29].

Footnotes

(1) "當年" here means "prime (壯年)", as in 《呂氏春秋•愛類》: "士有當年而不耕者, 則天下或受其饑矣." See 《漢語大詞典》. Shanghai: 上海辭書出版社, 2008, p.1390. Also see Remarks (II).

(2) "萬里" here means "far and wide (遠大)", as in 尉遲樞 《南楚新聞•崔鉉》 : "天邊心性架頭身, 欲擬飛騰未有因. 萬里碧霄終一去, 不知誰是解條人." Ibid., p.183.

(3) "戍" here means "defend (防守)", as in 《史記•陳涉世家》: "二世元年七月, 發閭左適戍漁陽." See 《漢語大字典》. Wuhan: 崇文書局, 2010, p.1501.

(4) "梁州" here refers to Langzhou in "Hanzhong (漢中)", a territory southwest of Guanhe (關河). See 脫脫, 《宋史》 Vol.89, 地理志. Taipei: 藝文印書館, 乾隆武英殿版, Book 2, p.1093. Also see Remarks (III).

(5) "匹馬" here means "單身一人 (singlehandedly)", as in 杜甫 《曲江三章章五句》 : "短衣匹馬隨李廣, 看射猛虎終殘年." See

《漢語大詞典》. Shanghai: 上海辭書出版社, 2008, p.949.

(6) "夢斷" here means "awakened from a dream (夢醒)", as in 李白《憶秦娥》: "簫聲咽, 秦娥夢斷秦樓月." Ibid., p.1189.

(7) "關河" here refers to Chang'an (長安) and its surrounding areas. See Remarks (III).

(8) "貂裘" here refers to "a fur coat (貂皮制成的衣裘)", as in 《淮南子•說山訓》 : "貂裘而雜, 不若狐裘而粹." See 《漢語大詞典》. Shanghai: 上海辭書出版社, 2008, p.1334.

(9) "鬢" here means "sideburn (臉旁靠近耳朵的頭髮)", as indicated in 《說文》: "鬢, 頰髮也." See《漢語大字典》. Wuhan: 崇文書局, 2010, p.4828.

(10) "天山" refers to the "Khangai Mountains (燕然山)", which now reside within Mongolia. See《漢語大詞典》. Shanghai: 上海辭書出版社, 2008, p.1406.

(11) "老" here means "death/pass away (死/逝)". See *Lyrics to the Immortal by the River* (《 臨江仙 • 庭院深深深幾許 》) in this book for further elaborations.

(12) "滄洲" here refers to "a place of reclusion (避世歸隱之地)". See *A Chanted Poem Upon a River* (《 江上吟 》) in this book for further elaborations.

(13) 脫脫,《宋史》Vol. 22 to 36. Taipei: 藝文印書館, 乾隆武英殿版, Book 1, pp.248-397.

(14)《宋史》Vol.395, 陸游傳. Ibid., Book 6, pp.4872-4873.

(15) Ibid..

(16) 張高寬,《宋詞大辭典》. Shenyang: 遼寧人民出版社, 1990, p.337.

(17) As in footnote (14).

(18) Ibid..

(19) 呂不韋,《呂氏春秋》Vol.21, 愛類. Hangzhou: 浙江書局, 光緒元年版, p.9b.

(20) 孫詒讓,《墨子閒詁》Book 2. Shanghai: 商務印書館, 1931, p.39.

(21) 謝選駿,《謝選駿全集》Vol.326. Raleigh: Lulu Press Inc., 2024, pp.528 & 530.

(22) 司馬遷,《史記》Vol.69, 蘇秦列傳. Hong Kong: 廣智書局, publication year unknown, Book 5, Vol.69, pp.1-2.

(23) As in footnote (14), p.4873.

(24) Ibid..

(25) Ibid..

(26) "跡" here means "功跡 (accomplishments)", as in 趙曄《吳越春秋•勾踐歸國外傳》: "霸王之跡, 自斯而起." See《漢語大詞典》. Shanghai: 上海辭書出版社, 2008, p.801.

(27) "近" here means "mediocre (平庸)", as in 徐幹《中論•爵祿》: "功小者, 其祿薄; 德近者, 其爵卑." Also, 陸游《上辛給事書》: "某

束髮好文, 才短識近." Ibid., p.730.

(28) As in footnote (23).

(29) 顧炎武,《亭林全集》Vol.4, 答子德書. Shanghai: 中華書局, publication year unknown, p.105.

A Jar of Wine
Fukuoka Art Museum
福岡市美術館
Fukuoka Japan

by KS Vincent Poon

Bibliography
參考書目

王力 ，《古代漢語》。北京: 中華書局 ，2001。

尤袤 ，《全唐詩話》。伊蔚堂 ，出版年地缺。

中華民國教育部 ，《 重編國語辭典修訂本 》 。臺灣: 臺灣學術網路第六版 ，2021。

司馬光 ，《資治通鑑》 ，胡三省注。 香港: 世界書局 ，1970。

司馬遷 ，《史記》。香港: 廣智書局 ，出版年份缺。

任中敏 ，《元曲三百首》。重慶: 中華書局 ，1945。

朱金城 ，《白居易集箋校》。上海: 上海古籍出版社 ，1988。

呂不韋 ，《呂氏春秋》。淅江書局 ，光緒元年版。

何休 ，《春秋公羊傳注疏》 。欽定四庫全書經部 ，乾隆四十年版。

何夢桂 ，《潛齋集》。欽定四庫全書集部 ，乾隆四十三年版。

沈采 ，《千金記》。出版年地缺。

李清照 ，《金石錄後序》。載趙明誠《金石錄》。欽定四庫全書史部 ，乾隆四十一年版。

吳楚材 ，《言文對照詳細註解古文觀止》。上海: 國學研究社出版，1949。

吳寬，《家藏集》。欽定四庫全書集部，乾隆四十一年版。

邵亨貞，《蟻術詞選》。出版年地缺。

周巽，《性情集》。欽定四庫全書集部，乾隆四十六年版。

洪适，《盤洲文集》。欽定四庫全書集部，乾隆四十六年版。

姚思廉，《梁書》。北京：中華書局，1973年。

耶律鑄，《雙溪醉隱集》。欽定四庫全書集部，乾隆四十六年版。

郁賢皓，《李白大辭典》。南寧：廣西教育出版社，1995。

唐圭璋，《全宋詞》。北京：中華書局，1999。

徐培均，《李清照集箋注》。上海：上海古籍出版社，2002。

孫詒讓，《墨子閒詁》。上海：商務印書館，1931。

張大復，《梅花草堂筆談》。上海：上海雜誌，1935。

張高寬，《宋詞大辭典》。瀋陽：遼寧人民出版社，1990。

張撝之，《中國歷代人名大辭典》。上海：上海古籍出版社，1999。

張傳璽，《中國古代史教學參考地圖集》。北京：北京大學出版社，1984。

曹丕，《與朝歌令吳質書》。載歐陽詢《藝文類聚》。欽定四庫全書子部，乾隆四十四年版。

曹寅，《全唐詩》。欽定四庫全書薈要集部，康熙四十六年版; 北京：中華書局，1979。

曹樹銘，《李清照詩詞文存》。臺北: 臺灣商務印書館，1992。

陳邦彥等，《康熙字典》。上海: 上海書店，1985。

陳邦瞻，《宋史紀事本末》。欽定四庫全書史部，乾隆四十九年版。

陳建，《皇明從信錄》。萬曆四十八年沈國元訂，出版年地缺。

陳振孫，《直齋書錄解題》。欽定四庫全書薈要史部，乾隆四十一年版。

脫脫，《宋史》。臺北: 藝文印書館，乾隆武英殿版。

黃庭堅，《豫章黃先生文集》。上海: 上海商務印書館，四部叢刊初編集部，縮印沈氏藏宋本。出版年份缺。

楊慎，《升菴集》。欽定四庫全書集部，乾隆四十三年版。

詹鍈，《李白全集校注匯釋集評》。天津: 百花文藝出版社，1996。

漢語大字典編輯委員會，《漢語大字典》。武漢: 崇文書局，2010。

漢語大詞典編輯委員會，《漢語大詞典》。上海: 上海辭書出版社，2008。

趙明誠，《金石錄》。欽定四庫全書史部，乾隆四十一年版。

趙曉輝，《李清照》。北京: 五洲傳播出版社，2005。

臧勵龢，《中國古今地名大辭典》。臺北: 臺灣商務印書館，1966。

劉向，《列仙傳》。欽定四庫全書子部，乾隆四十六年版。

劉辰翁，《須溪集》。欽定四庫全書集部，乾隆四十六年版。

劉昫，《舊唐書》。臺灣: 臺灣中華書局，1971。

鄭振鐸，《中國文學史》。上海: 上海商務印書館，1932。

葉盛，《水東日記》。欽定四庫全書子部，乾隆四十三年版。

歐陽修，《新唐書》。北京: 中華書局，1975。

蕭統，《昭明文選》。崇文書局，同治八年版。出版地缺。

謝逸，《溪堂集》。欽定四庫全書集部，乾隆四十六年版。

謝選駿，《謝選駿全集》。Raleigh: Lulu Press Inc.，2024。

魏收，《魏書》。北京:中華書局，1974。

顧炎武，《亭林全集》。上海: 中華書局，出版年份缺。

顧嗣立，《元詩選》。秀野草堂，出版年地缺。

蘇軾，《東坡全集》。欽定四庫全書集部，乾隆四十六年版。

蘇軾，《蘇東坡集》。長沙: 商務印書館，1939。

酈道元，《水經注》。上海: 中華書局，1936。

KS Vincent Poon，*Calligraphy Meets Philosophy - Talk 3* (《尚語 • 第三話》)。Toronto: The Senseis，2024。

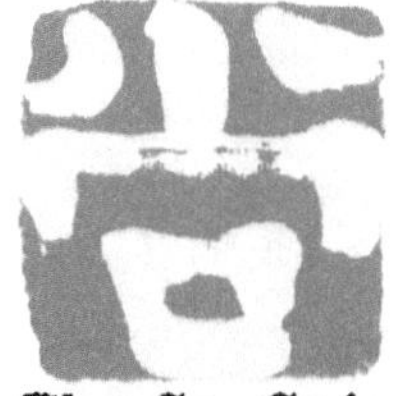

尚尚齋